EARLY CHILDHOOD EDUCATION REDEFINED

GW00771022

Probing the shortcomings of contemporary early years provision, whilst offering practical and informed solutions, *Early Childhood Education Redefined* at once celebrates the progress made in this field since the publication of the 'Start Right Report' (1994), whilst also calling for further changes to ensure that all children are able to 'start right', to become effective, independent learners.

Developing and emphasising the importance of concepts which have become overlooked within modern educational policy and practice, yet which remain key to our children's development, this book considers how elements such as attachment and love; movement and exercise; and language and talk may be better integrated into early years practice via the three main vectors of parenting, the curriculum, and pedagogy. From a revised curriculum from birth to seven renamed Key Stage 1, to a greater emphasis on formative assessment combined with standardised tests, and the promotion of pedagogies including *purposeful play*, *in the moment planning* and *attachment theory*, chapters build on the principles set out in the 'Start Right Report' and take into consideration the research and reflection developed over the last quarter of a decade.

Reopening a vital debate and challenging governments, education providers, parents and professionals to re-define what young children need to grow, develop and learn in our contemporary society, this timely response to the 'Start Right Report' is essential reading for all those involved in early years research, education and care.

Pat Preedy is Adjunct Professor at Curtin University, Western Australia and Educational Consultant.

Kay Sanderson is Project Lead, Review and Development of KG Curriculum United Arab Emirates, Ministry of Education Dubai and Cognition Education, New Zealand.

Sir Christopher Ball is former Chairman of the WAVE Trust, UK, and author of *Start Right: The Importance of Early Learning* (RSA, 1994).

EARLY CHILDHOOD EDUCATION REDEFINED

Reflections and Recommendations on the Impact of Start Right

Edited by Pat Preedy, Kay Sanderson and Sir Christopher Ball

Routledge
Taylor & Francis Group

LONDON AND NEW YORK

First published 2019
by Routledge
2 Park Square, Milton Park, Abingdon, Oxon OX14 4RN

and by Routledge
711 Third Avenue, New York, NY 10017

Routledge is an imprint of the Taylor & Francis Group, an informa business

British Library Cataloguing-in-Publication Data
A catalogue record for this book is available from the British Library

Library of Congress Cataloging-in-Publication Data
A catalog record for this book has been requested

ISBN: 978-0-8153-8026-9 (hbk)
ISBN: 978-0-8153-8027-6 (pbk)
ISBN: 978-1-351-21366-0 (ebk)

Typeset in Bembo
by Apex CoVantage, LLC

Printed and bound in Great Britain by
TJ International Ltd, Padstow, Cornwall

To my dear late husband Keith and daughter Laura who have supported and encouraged me throughout my career.
Pat Preedy

To my husband Lee and our children, Zoe and Zak, who inspire me in every way.
Kay Sanderson

To my wife Wendy and our children who taught me most about the early years of life.
Sir Christopher Ball

CONTENTS

ABOUT THE AUTHORS AND EDITORS

Pat Preedy has had a long and distinguished career in education, which includes being a global Chief Academic Officer for early childhood education, Executive Principal of a school catering for pupils from 3 months to 18 years with boarding, Head Teacher of one of the first Beacon Schools in the UK and a school inspector. She completed her Masters in Educational Management, particularly investigating how schools can work in partnership with parents, and a doctorate in Education. As Honorary Research Consultant for Tamba (Twins and Multiple Births Association) Pat has conducted extensive research into meeting the educational needs of multiple birth children. She was also part of the team that developed the performance indicators in primary schools' value added baseline assessments (University of Durham CEM centre). Currently Pat is an adjunct professor at Curtin University (W. Australia) and is involved in conducting a range of research including the Movement for Learning Project developed through Loughborough University and Parents as Play Partners Project developed through Middlesex University (Dubai).

Kay Sanderson (SFHEA) is an experienced academic, education leader and mother, with a PhD in Education Research, PGCE and an MBA in International Management. She has worked in all sectors of education over the last 20 years, including early years, primary, secondary and tertiary. Her most recent role was that of Programme Coordinator of Education at Middlesex University Dubai, where she was responsible for overseeing and lecturing on all programmes and was instrumental in introducing the first UK accredited BA (Hons) Early Childhood Studies to Dubai, United Arab Emirates. Kay is currently working as the Project Lead for the *Review and Development of the Kindergarten Curriculum in the UAE*.

She is passionate about early childhood education and has been instrumental in developing and promoting innovative research projects within the region. Her early childhood interests have enabled her to travel extensively throughout the Gulf region and wider world, to both initiate conferences and deliver presentations in the areas of parental engagement, play and movement. She has also developed early childhood teacher training programmes for those in remote communities and been has instrumental in building schools in the Tandrang region of Nepal.

As an experienced coach she has developed educational coaching materials to support leaders in determining their actions through reflection and goal setting, enabling them to influence those within their circle to promote the developmental growth of teachers and children.

Sir Christopher Ball was born in 1935 and educated at Oxford after National Service with the Parachute Regiment. He was a lecturer in Comparative Linguistics at London University, then Fellow in English at Lincoln College, Oxford. He served with the Council for National Academic Awards and was formerly Warden of Keble College, Oxford, and Chairman of the Board of the National Advisory Body for Public Sector Higher Education. He is married, with six (adult) children, and eight grandchildren.

His service with CNAA and BTEC, as Visiting Professor in Education at Leeds Polytechnic, Governor of Templeton College, Oxford, and Manchester Polytechnic, Chairman of Brathay Hall Trust, and his experience in Higher, Continuing and Further Education, in Development Training, and Education-Industry links, both in the UK and overseas, is represented in *Fitness for Purpose* (1985), *Aim Higher* (1989), *Higher Education into the 1990s* (with Heather Eggins, 1989), *More Means Different* (1990), *Learning Pays* (1991), *Sharks and Splashes!: The Future of Education and Employment* (1991) and *Profitable Learning* (1992), amongst others.

President of the Association of Colleges of Further and Higher Education from 1990–1992, Chairman of the Education-Industry Forum (Industry Matters, RSA) from 1989–1990, and of the National Institute for Careers Education and Counselling (1989–1992), he has worked with the CBI Education and Training Affairs Committee and Price Waterhouse. As the former RSA Fellow in Continuing Education and the RSA's Director of Learning, he directed several projects, including one on Early Learning, of which the report, entitled 'Start Right', was published in March 1994. In June 1994 he became the founding Chairman of the National Advisory Council for Careers and Educational Guidance. He was appointed Chancellor of the University of Derby in 1995, and was the founder, and is now one of the Patrons, of the National Campaign for Learning. He was education adviser to The Esmée Fairbairn Charitable Trust from 1991–2000, and Chairman of The Achievement Trust until 2008.

In recent years he has been vice-chairman of the Jigsaw Group of Nurseries (1998–2004), founder and chairman (now patron) of The Talent Foundation (1999), and chairman of The Global University Alliance (2000–2004), WAVE (2004–2007) and Down's Syndrome Education Int. (2009–2015). His interests include all aspects of human learning – especially 'early learning', lifelong learning, brain science, motivation, self-esteem and the exploration of the limits of human potential. At the age of 70 he partly retired from public life to devote himself to a small number of specific high-value projects – as well as running marathons, writing poetry, and helping small charities raise funds.

Ruth Churchill Dower is Director of Earlyarts, an award-winning training and research organisation, dedicated to enabling children's arts and creativity to unlock their greatest learning potential. Ruth supports hundreds of educators each year as a trainer, consultant, author, speaker and thought leader, with a specialist focus on how creative strategies can nurture our learning and leadership development.

Ruth is a Fellow of the Royal Society of the Arts (FRSA), a founding member of the Cultural Learning Alliance and the national Early Years Strategy Group, an associate member of Small Size, an accredited Relational Dynamics Coach, a paraglider pilot and a qualified Mountain Survival First Aider.

In 2009, Ruth won the Ogunte Women's Social Leadership Awards for her work in building Earlyarts to make real change happen through creative learning. Through Earlyarts consultancy practice, Ruth has worked with major international clients such as Sharjah Museums Department, Independent Schools Association, Al Jalila Cultural Centre for Children (Dubai), Arts Council England, Arts Council Ireland and National Museums Liverpool. Ruth has also been a visiting lecturer at Huddersfield University, the University of Hertfordshire, the University of East Anglia and Norwich School of Art and Design.

Rebecca Duncombe is currently a Teaching Fellow in the School of Sport, Exercise and Health Sciences at Loughborough University. Prior to this she was a research associate in the Institute of Youth Sport and worked on a number of projects related to engaging young people in and through sport and Physical Education. More recently, she has focused on physical development in the early years and, over the last 2 years, has worked in collaboration with Pat Preedy to develop *Movement for Learning*: a daily programme of exercises designed to be delivered to the whole class and aimed at children in Foundation Stage and Year 1. She was a primary school teacher earlier in her career and recently completed the Institute for Neuro Physiological Psychology's Postgraduate course in INNP (primitive reflex) theory.

Sally Goddard Blythe MSc. is the international Director of The Institute for Neuro-Physiological Psychology (INPP) in Chester and is responsible for the content and standardisation of training in the INPP method throughout the world.

Sally is the author of seven books and other published papers on child development and neuro-developmental factors in specific learning difficulties, including: *Reflexes, Learning and Behaviour, The Well Balanced Child, Raising Happy Healthy Children, The Genius of Natural Childhood* and *Attention, Balance and Coordination – the A,B,C of Learning Success* – a reference source for all professionals involved in child development and education. She is the developer and author of a screening test and developmental movement programme for use in schools, *Assessing Neuromotor Readiness for Learning,* and a screening test for clinicians and health practitioners.

Rosie Hamilton McGinty is the founder of 'A Winning Attitude Coaching and Training Program' and author of nine self-help books based on Character and Attitude Development. A motivational and after-dinner speaker and well-known author, Rosie is particularly interested in supporting children and their families. Rosie's past experience includes setting up and running a small school for expatriate children in Nigeria.

Rosie's existing titles include *A Winning Attitude, Believe in Yourself, Simple Steps to Happiness* and *Stress in the Workplace*. Her over-arching mantra revolves around bringing out the best in people. She believes that a positive and 'a winning attitude' can help people to conquer their individual problems and resolve personal conflicts. Her new educational programme with Professor Pat Preedy has been developed to assist schools and parents to 'Bring out the Best in our Children'. See more at: http://awinningattitude.com/

Karen Morris is a Senior Lecturer in Childhood Studies at the University of Winchester. Her background is in educational psychology and she has extensive experience of working with children and families. Her research interests focus on motivation and well-being and she is currently undertaking a doctorate in Educational Psychology at UCL. In 2015, Karen published her first book, *Promoting Positive Behaviour in the Early Years*.

Samantha Steed's teaching career spans over 20 years with 10 years as a School leader both in the UK and overseas. She was Head of Early Years and Deputy Head teacher at Prospect House, Putney, before taking on the roles of Headteacher at both Haresfoot School, Berkhamsted, and then of Berkhamsted School Pre-Prep. She moved to Dubai in September 2015 to become the founding Principal of Ranches Primary School, a five-form entry FS1 to Year 6 British curriculum school.

Samantha originally trained as a teacher, specialising in Early Years at Froebel College, Roehampton, gaining the BA (with QTS); more recently, she was awarded a Masters of Education (with Distinction) from Winchester University, researching Wellbeing and Happiness Education.

Samantha is an Early Years specialist and has spoken widely at conferences and on training courses both in the UK and the UAE. She writes regularly on a range of educational issues and is a passionate advocate for the retention of play in Early Years education.

Helen Wright has led outstanding schools in the UK and Australia for over 13 years, and was Vice-Chair of the UK Independent Schools' Council from 2011–2012. She was *Tatler*'s 'Best Head of a Public School' in 2011, and is noted for her challenging views on futures thinking in education; she is regularly asked to speak at, and chair sessions at, international conferences. Since 2014 she has focused on the field of international education, advising schools and educational organisations on change management. She particularly enjoys coaching and challenging school leaders across the world, from early years settings to pre-university programmes, and she contributes annually to the Australian Independent Schools' Leadership Programme for New Principals. Her book, *Powerful Schools: How Schools Can Be Drivers of Social and Global Mobility*, was published in 2016. She is a non-executive director on a number of boards in the UK and abroad, from ed-tech start-ups to national organisations and international schools.

INTRODUCTION

Pat Preedy

I have always wanted to be a teacher. As a young child play usually revolved around school, taking the register and writing sums on the chalkboard. I still remember my first teacher and many others with great fondness and gratitude. It is thanks to them and to the wonderful support that I received from my parents and family that I also became a teacher and have had a fulfilling career in education, including being a headteacher, chief academic officer, inspector, consultant and researcher.

I am passionate about early childhood education and have spent much of my career trying to provide what young children really need to thrive. Rather than blindly accept initiatives that are frequently based on little evidence, I embarked on a pathway of research. My recent work has involved working alongside talented colleagues and fellow researchers, including Dr Kay Sanderson, who is a co-editor and contributor to this book. Dr Kay and I developed and conducted action research through the Parents and Carers as Play Partners Project detailed in Chapter 6. Evaluation of this study confirmed my view that childhood play and parental engagement are vitally important to children's development and learning and should not be lost in today's fast-paced world of technology and curriculum reforms.

This and other research, combined with my passion for early childhood education, led me over the past 10 years to become increasingly concerned that the Early Years Foundation Stage does not adequately cover the actual stage of early childhood – from birth to 7 years, and is causing a barrier between Reception and Year One. Late one evening I looked at my bookshelves and reached for the original *Start Right Report* (1994) by Sir Christopher Ball. As I read it I reflected on the sea-change that it had heralded putting the early years to the forefront of the minds of politicians and the world. The words of wisdom, underpinned by the rigorous research led by Professor Kathy Sylva, were still powerful. However, subsequent revisions of the Early Years Foundation Stage (EYFS) seemed to have lost some of the original message, such as the inclusion of science as an area of learning. Assessment using the Early Years Foundation Stage Profile was now dominating the system with the production of an enormous amount of data that were highly suspect with regard to validity and reliability. In addition, the current EYFS framework did not sufficiently take into account changes in the modern world, including language learning, technology and the engagement of parents. I wondered if Sir Christopher was still with us because he must be in his eighties!?

After an Internet search I managed to find a contact number and tentatively waited as I listened to the phone ringing. Suddenly, an authoritative voice stated, 'Sir Christopher Ball speaking.' I was so surprised that Sir Christopher himself had answered the phone that I blurted out, 'I wasn't sure if you were still alive!' Sir Christopher has since translated this into me saying, 'I thought you were dead!!!!' Once I had apologised, Sir Christopher listened with interest to my views and ideas and invited me to meet him. It was immediately as though we had known each other for a long time – no need for lengthy explanations. From these conversations grew the idea of re-defining early childhood education and providing educators and the wider world with new information about what we need to do to ensure that our children *start right*.

We then progressed to writing this book, which includes contributions from colleagues and researchers who are well respected in the field of education. We are proposing some bold steps including the implementation of a new Early Years Framework that I have developed, detailed in Chapter 2. Sir Christopher has been supportive, challenging and encouraging. The proceeds of our work will go to the *British Heart Foundation* as we are keen that every aspect of this book will make a positive difference to others.

I am pleased to report that Sir Christopher is very much with us and, as in 1994 he is not afraid to speak his mind and to lead change for the benefit of our youngest children. Please join us in re-defining early childhood education and enabling young children to *start right*.

Reference

Ball, C. (1994). *Start Right: The Importance of Early Learning*. London: RSA.

1

START RIGHT REVISITED

Sir Christopher Ball

Start Right, The Importance of Early Learning, was published by the RSA in 1994 –
almost a quarter of a century ago. The Foreword, contributed by three leaders from
the worlds of social service, business and industry, and the care and resettlement of
offenders, asserted that:

> This Report presents a challenge to the nation, to parents, educators, employers,
> parliament – indeed to our society as a whole. It demonstrates the impor-
> tance of early learning as a preparation for effective education to promote
> social welfare and social order, and to develop a world-class workforce. It
> shows how countries benefit which provide good pre-school education for
> their children. . . . The Report examines good practice. . . . It finds that the
> key factors are a curriculum which encourages 'active learning', well-trained
> staff of the highest quality, and the involvement of parents in a triangle of
> care involving parents, professionals and society. Each requires attention if we
> are to provide our young children with the start they need for learning, for
> work and for life.
>
> The time is ripe for significant change. The Prime Minister has personally
> responded to the growing public concern about provision of nursery educa-
> tion. The Report argues that this should be among our highest priorities. It
> squarely confronts the problem of resources, and offers a new and unexpected
> solution. We, too, believe that 'no child born after the year 2000 should be
> deprived of the opportunity and support for effective early learning'.
>
> The Report, containing seventeen recommendations for action, is contro-
> versial and provocative. It will stimulate a wide-ranging and lively debate. But
> we hope that this will not delay an effective response from the Government
> and others to whom it is addressed. All children should be enabled to start right.
>
> *(Ball 1994, p. 6)*

Start Right attracted considerable attention from the press, parliament and the public. It earned front-page headlines in the London evening papers when it was published. Welcomed by the Prime Minister (John Major) – and then immediately dismissed by the Secretary of State for Education – it provoked an ongoing debate about the importance of early learning, its nature, its inextricable relationship with child-care, the appropriate social provision required, and the need for providers and practitioners of the highest quality. The five major findings won widespread support: that good early learning is the foundation-stone for a well-lived life; that the *triangle of care* provided by parents, professionals and society as a whole is essential in early childhood; that the provision must be of the highest quality if it is to be fully effective ('good enough is not good enough'); that progress is possible and resources can be found – provided the political will can be harnessed to the task; and that to further neglect the needs of the most vulnerable members of our society – young children, especially those from a deprived or disadvantaged background – would be nothing short of a national disgrace.

The nation, and its leaders, responded to this challenge. Over the next few years most of the 17 recommendations were discussed and addressed and many of them were implemented – for example, *12. The Government should immediately prepare legislation to create by 1999 a statutory responsibility for the provision of free, high-quality, half-day pre-school education for all children from the age of three, in an integrated context of day-care.* The programme named *Sure Start*, perhaps echoing the title of the Report, went a long way towards providing what was needed. I commend it. But the authors of this book, myself included, feel the time has now come to revisit, not just the *Start Right* Report, but more importantly the whole subject of 'the importance of early learning', to reconsider and review what still remains to be done, what has been done – but not well enough, and what further things now need to be done in the light of our learning and experience since 1994.

I identify three major areas of weakness in the provision for early childhood in our society – in spite of all that has been achieved over the past 20 years. They are: the education and support of parents, the curriculum, and the pedagogy for children from birth to 7 years. (*Curriculum* means *what* the child should be learning, and being taught; *pedagogy* means *how* the child should be learning, and being taught. The world of education – and society at large – is obsessed with curriculum, but sadly neglects pedagogy. And yet in human learning *how* one learns governs *what* is learned.)

The education and support of parents is a subject – and a challenge – that deserves several books to itself. And many such books have been written. For my generation the authoritative text was Benjamin Spock's *Baby and Child Care* (1946), which taught us useful wisdom like: 'children know best about food: parents know best about sleep', 'if your child seems unwell, don't worry – it's probably not serious – but ask your doctor about it anyway', 'keep your word – never make a promise or a threat that you are not prepared to honour' and 'support your partner – never allow the child to divide the parents'... Raising six children, my wife and I found precepts like these helpful, and they have stood the test of time.

Today, I teach (when given the chance) the simple mnemonic of NESTLE, while role-modelling the nursing mother with her baby at her breast: Nurture, Exercise, Stimulation, Talk, Love, Environment – this list offers a summary of the agenda for parents to learn and practise. (NESTLE is not a reference to dried milk!) Parents need to learn the art of nurture (as opposed to nature, which comes naturally) in both the narrow sense of 'nourishment' and the broader one embracing the whole subject of child-rearing. They should ensure that the child is provided with opportunities for healthy exercise, indoors and outdoors. They need to provide appropriate stimulation for the imagination, without the risk of overstimulation or over-reliance on technology. Children need talk – and time and tenderness: parents who are too busy to converse with (and listen to) their child are failing to do their job. Love seems obvious, but not all parents understand what love means: it means acceptance, care and trust. We all need and want to be loved in a way that combines these three strands, to be accepted – even when our behaviour is unacceptable, to be cared for – come what may, and to be trusted – even when we have proved ourselves untrustworthy. The art of love is not an easy one to master, and maintain. As for the environment, one of the most important parental tasks is to provide the child with an environment (both indoors and outdoors) that is both stimulating and safe. For most children today the external environment offers neither an adequate challenge of adventure nor real safety. We have sacrificed the well-being of our children to the false god of the private motor-car.

In the chapters that follow, contributors who speak with more experience and authority than I, develop this theme of the education and support that parents need today. I especially note Chapters 5 and 6, which highlight the importance of parenting and ways that parents can engage with their children particularly through play. I hope that one of the outcomes of the publication of this book might be a revival of interest in the subject, and the possibility of a national debate of the question: what do parents need to know? However, *knowledge* is the easy part: sound *values*, appropriate *attitudes*, the *skills* of child-rearing and the benefits of *experience* prove to be even more important to those embarking on the long and challenging journey of parenthood.

We postponed our great project of the adoption of (four) children, whose natural parents were unable (or unwilling) to care for them, until we had produced – and learned from – two 'home-made' babies. The experience of caring for these two 'training children' (as they are sometimes called in the family to this day) helped us to learn what we needed to know. One of the wisest things I have ever heard is the advice of the (wonderful) midwife, shortly after the birth of our first child, when I was left in charge of a new baby and a sleeping wife, feeling totally unprepared for the responsibility; 'Don't worry, Sir Christopher – if you don't know what to do, and your wife doesn't either, the baby will know!' Children often, but not always, know the answer, when parents are perplexed. We should be ready to learn from them.

A delicate and sensitive issue for parents – and for those who write about parenthood – is the separate roles of the mother and the father, and the value to the child of two role models, of either sex, who stay together at least until the task of child-rearing is completed. I wrote in *Start Right*,

> In the present state of knowledge, there is a case not so much for reasserting the traditional model of parenthood (with its pre-determined gender-specific roles), as for promoting a modern version of it (providing flexibility of role), with parents who contract to stay together at least until the (youngest) child reaches the age of parenthood, and who honour the contract.
>
> *(Ball 1994, paragraph 5.8)*

Interviewed shortly afterwards, I was asked whether I seriously expected couples to wait until their youngest had reached the age of 15 before going their separate ways, if they wished to. I explained that I had meant the age of normal, responsible parenthood – which then was approaching (and now has almost reached) twice that figure! However, the Marriage Foundation informs us that today only 50 per cent of children will still be living with both (married) birth-parents, when they reach the age of 15, while the figures for co-habiting couples are even lower.

Paragraphs 5.8 and 5.9 caused some difficulty to my colleagues, who in some cases dissociated themselves from this part of the Report, and to some of its readers who did not agree with statements promoting the importance of fathers and concerned by the high risks associated with single parenthood and broken parenthood. But I stand by them. My concern is the needs of children, not the convenience of adults. Of particular interest today is the question of distinct roles for fathers and mothers. My personal experience has been of the 'traditional' model of the father as bread-winner, and the mother managing the home and family. It worked for us. But, today, there is a wide variety of different models to study and ponder, including shared roles, alternating roles and the converse of the traditional model, as well as single parenthood, broken homes and complex multiple step-families. Research and common sense tells us that a child's life chances diminish with each step of the way from the traditional model of the nuclear genetic family, to adoption, fostering and institutional care. I wish it were otherwise. We need more research on the new patterns of child-rearing that are becoming commonplace. When I wrote *Start Right*, I tried to argue from the child's point of view, as best as I could ascertain it. It is all too easy for adults to assume that what is convenient for them will be good enough for the children in their care. This is often not the case.

Social norms are valuable; we should not discard them carelessly. Men and women are different, both by nature and in their learned behaviour, and children seem to benefit from having both a mother and a father, if possible. It used to be said, 'Mothers are for care; fathers are for play.' The mother's instinct is to keep the child safe; the father's to encourage adventure and risk. The mother holds the baby to her breast, or on her lap; the father throws the baby in the air (and catches it) – which is why my role-modelling of the nursing mother (see above) always amuses the audience! In a century and a nation rightly determined to give the fullest equality of opportunity to both genders, we must be careful not to assume that they are identical – especially when it comes to the great task of child-rearing. Observe the babies, and ask the children. Their instinctive knowledge and attitudes deserve careful consideration, and respect. I hope these preliminary paragraphs, and this book, may serve to stimulate a wider national debate on parenthood, to enable us to identify more securely what is best for the children, and to provide appropriate education and training, in both the science and the arts of parenting, to promote good practice across the whole of our society. There is no greater, or more pressing, national challenge today.

What would good practice look like in a society that responded to this challenge, I wonder? As a first step – to launch the debate, perhaps – I propose ten guidelines for our grandchildren to ponder and evaluate:

1   Choose a reliable, long-term partner (listen to both head and heart – and study the online NVQ on 'preparing for parenthood', which is a prerequisite for qualifying for child benefit payments) [I wish!];
2   Before starting a pregnancy ensure that you are both in good health, have a good enough home for the baby to share with you, and are jointly practising the discipline of NESTLE (see above) in preparation for the birth;
3   Once the baby is born, NESTLE your child, encouraging the virtues of a patterned life, good habits and human kindness;
4   Teach by example – demonstrate the virtues of self-reliance, strong families and the learning habit;
5   Foster curiosity and independence, while always providing a framework of security and protection for the young child;
6   Learn to practise 'tough love' (study for a vocational course focusing on effective parenting);
7   Create a supportive partnership with your child's school(s), the teachers and your friends (and theirs), to develop the 'triangle of care' (see the *Start Right* Report) that is essential for good long-term nurture of the young;
8, 9 and 10 I leave for the reader (and our grandchildren) to identify. The elderly know much – but they don't know it all!

However, ignorance of – or failure to learn and observe – these simple guidelines contributes not a little to a range of social evils in Britain (and elsewhere) today: child neglect, foetal alcohol syndrome and eating disorders, conditions of anxiety and OCD, lives that seem both 'unexamined' (as Socrates deplored) and undisciplined, learned incompetence, dependency and educational failure, ill health and poverty, crime, addiction and self-harm, obesity, drug abuse and early death… The education, training and support of parents really matters to us all. But it matters most to our children – and to their children.

The early years curriculum was summed up in the phrase 'purposeful play' in *Start Right* and set out authoritatively by Professor Kathy Sylva in greater detail in Appendix E (Glossary and Curriculum). In Chapter 2 of this book Pat Preedy proposes a revised Early Years Framework that replaces the current EYFS with a

Key Stage One that covers birth to age 7. It takes into account changes in our society and the latest research. I commend it.

The appropriate pedagogy should, of course, go hand in hand with the curriculum. This principle underpins effective education at any age or stage of learning – since *what* we learn, as every experienced teacher (or learner) knows, depends critically on *how* we learn it, and *how* it is imparted to us. Without good pedagogy, the best curriculum will remain inert.

What is effective pedagogy? Most learners tell us that they want a teacher who loves them – accepts them, cares for them and trusts them – and who challenges them to become their best selves. The task of the teacher is to help ordinary people – like us, the authors, and you, the readers, of this book, and those in our care – to live extraordinary lives. I like the formulation of *warm, demanding adults* as a first approximation of what a teacher – or parent, or leader – should try to become. We all need to surround ourselves with 'warm, demanding adults' throughout our lives, if we are to make the most of them.

Good pedagogy starts with the requirement of providing a good role model for those in our care. Walk the talk. Lead, and teach, by example. We are social creatures and learn by imitation. Wordsworth said of the small child, 'As if his whole vocation/ Were endless imitation' (1807). Good teachers understand that successful learning is critically dependent on two qualities: the desire to learn, and belief in one's own capability to learn (whatever is required). And these qualities are themselves learnable – and teachable. If you don't want to learn to dance the tango, for example, and know you'd be no good at it, you probably won't ever try. *Experto credite!* So the first task of the teacher is to develop the learner's qualities of determination and resilience, and of confidence and self-belief. One useful definition of 'readiness to learn' is that all-important combination of eagerness and self-confidence, which is the pre-requisite of success in learning, work and life. Those who have mastered these qualities will put in the practice that is necessary for any worthwhile learning challenge – reading, numeracy, music or dancing, and the rest (the curriculum).

Good teachers understand the distinction between *learning disabilities* and *learning disorders*. In the world of mental health, experts distinguish between mental disabilities (like Down's Syndrome or autism) and mental disorders (like acute anxiety, phobias or OCD). The former are (largely) innate, the latter learned (though some of us may be pre-disposed to adopt these damaging conditions). Indeed some people (I am one) argue that, while mental disabilities are best diagnosed and treated by the medical professions, mental disorders should be seen as the province of the teaching profession, not the doctors. Cognitive Behavioural Therapy is education, not medicine. As Nelson Mandela (1994) said, 'No one is born hating another person because of the colour of their skin, or their background, or their religion. People must learn to hate, and if they can learn to hate, they can be taught to love.' And that is our job.

We lack a taxonomy of learning disorders, but it isn't hard to find examples of common types, like lack of motivation or self-confidence, inattention or distraction, carelessness, and suchlike. These learning disorders feel as if they are no more than a normal (if regrettable) part of the human condition, of course. Everyone suffers from them to a certain extent. But they are learned behaviours – and we can learn to reduce them, or even avoid them altogether. Studying my own efforts to become a first-class solver of *The Times* daily crossword (part of the curriculum for my ninth decade), I notice three prevailing faults (bad habits or 'learning disorders'): careless inattention to the task – I often misread the clues; 'tunnel vision' – I convince myself that the clue must be of a certain type (a hidden anagram, perhaps), when in fact it is of a quite different type ('double definition' or 'concealed word', for example); and a shameful tendency to give up trying to solve a clue, when only a little more intellectual effort would have brought success. I am training myself to avoid, or at least reduce the impact of, these bad habits.

An interesting example of learning disorder is found in the Honey and Mumford theory of learning styles (1982), which suggests that people tend to favour one of four styles of learning: activist ('let me do it!'), pragmatic ('what's the point of learning this?'), reflective ('I need to think about it') and theoretic ('how does this fit into what I already know?'). My own preferred learning style is the fourth, as the reader may already be able to guess! (Most readers will probably be able to identify their preferred learning style from this brief description of the four types.) Those, like me, who use this system to help learners understand their own preferred style find both that most students can readily recognise their favoured style of learning and that they enjoy the discovery – and finding others like them.

But it seems clear that the most efficient and effective learners are those who can draw upon all four 'learning styles' to help them master the challenges of the curriculum. Therefore, I argue that those of us with a distinctive 'preferred learning style' (like me!) have a mild learning disorder. We need gentle encouragement to experiment with the other three approaches until we are as adept with the 'unfavoured styles' as we are with our habitual approach to learning. The key point is that learning styles are 'learned behaviours': in principle, if we have learned them, we could unlearn them.

The new brain-sciences are providing many interesting and valuable insights into the human brain, its development and its operation. One idea is that we have 'two brains': a rational, analytical tool for solving problems carefully and slowly, and a rapid response system providing immediate (and often valuable) insights and solutions. I am seeking to learn to use both in finding solutions to crossword clues, although my education, habit and culture favour the former. As a result, I can do *The Times* crossword a good deal faster, and more accurately, than I could 20 years ago. Practice helps, of course – but two brains are better than one. Failing to harness both is a common learning disorder.

One of the most important questions in the science of pedagogy is how much of learning success (or failure) is due to the brains we are born with (our innate talents), how much is the result of our nurture and education (the learning environment) and how much depends on the personal choices we make, as we grow and develop? Social attitudes (and a strong strand of educational tradition, alas) seem to identify the brains we are born with as the most influential. My own view is different – and a good deal more hopeful. I believe that the combination of nurture and education and personal choices can in many (perhaps most) cases outweigh any disadvantage we may have been born with. With very few exceptions, probably rather less than 5 per cent, we are all born with brains that might enable us to become, say, university graduates, if that is what we want, and if we are given appropriate support and help throughout our development (nurture and education) at home, in school and university. Early childhood is for many the turning point – which is why our early learning is so important, and all children should be enabled to start right. The sad truth is: we are not born stupid – but many of us learn to behave stupidly.

One of the reasons for such an unorthodox view lies in the plasticity of the brain. The human brain seems to be able to respond to the demands made upon it, for example in the realm of language-learning: those whose first language is that of a minority group (like Finnish or Hungarian, for example) master one (or more) of the world's major languages without real difficulty, regardless of *measured intelligence* – which, anyway, seems to be an instrument of doubtful scientific validity. The idea of people having *limited intelligence* seems to be disproved by countless examples of individuals who learn what they choose to, or need to, when circumstances dictate it. Thousands of children failed the 11+ examination during the twentieth century – and went on to gain degrees at the Open University and elsewhere. Changes in patterns of employment and educational expectations show that (most) humans have brains that can respond to unlimited challenge. Or, to put it another way, most of us – most of the time – only engage a part of the extraordinary potential of our brains. (I plead guilty.)

I seek to challenge the education profession to re-engage with the science of pedagogy, to reclaim the realm of 'learning disorders' from the medical profession, to redefine the concept of learning readiness, to learn to be sceptical of genetic explanations of talent (or apparent lack of it), and to help all students understand the extraordinary potential of their remarkable brains – and, therefore, the infinite possibilities of learning. I believe that (with very few exceptions) anyone can be, or do, or know (and master), what other humans have been able to learn or achieve or become. We might all become poets or professors, lawyers or leaders, singers or scientists – or even dancers! – if we were to muster the necessary determination and self-belief, and put in the practice. Helping students to do that is the task of good pedagogy. It starts in the home, and nursery school. Which is why this book has been written – so that, as far as possible, every child may be enabled to start right upon the great human journey of learning to develop our extraordinary potential.

> None of these things will happen without an assertion of political will, accompanied by popular support and directed through decisive leadership. The translation of national aspirations into reality cannot be achieved by government alone. It requires the co-operation, effort and enterprise of many agencies and all parts of society. Political will inevitably reflects the general will of society. But political leadership can shape the general will. Progress

is possible. Nations have learned to free slaves, end child labour, extend the franchise to women. We can decide to stop neglecting the early education of our children. We may expect a range of economic, social and personal benefits if we do so. But these are not the most compelling reasons for action. We should act because it is right. Our children's children will not readily forgive us, if we decline to face the challenge, or fail.

(*Start Right, paragraph 8.15*)

References

Ball, C. (1994). *Start Right: The Importance of Early Learning*. London: RSA.

Honey, P. & Mumford, A. (1982). *Manual of Learning Styles*. London: P. Honey.

Mandela, N. (1994). *Long Walk to Freedom: The Autobiography of Nelson Mandela*. Boston, MA: Little, Brown and Company.

Spock, B. (1946). *Baby and Child Care*. New York: Duell, Sloan and Pearce.

Wordsworth, W. (1807). Ode. Intimations of Immortality from Recollections of Early Childhood in *Poems, in Two Volumes*. London: Longman.

2

ROOTS TO GROW WINGS TO FLY

Re-defining early childhood education

Pat Preedy

In 1953, Hodding Carter referred to a quote from an unnamed woman that high-lighted the importance of giving our children roots and wings – our main aim as early years educators. The Start Right Report (Ball, 1994) presented strong evidence that good early childhood education gives children lasting social and educational benefits. As a headteacher of an infant school at the time I, along with many others, welcomed *Start Right* as it trumpeted the importance of early learning underpinned by a curriculum that recognised and supported a pedagogy based on play, and the importance of working in partnership with parents. I was inspired to write my masters dissertation on ways in which early years teachers can develop a partnership with parents that focuses on the child's development and learning rather than ways in which parents can help in school. It felt that at last we would be able to give all children the wings they needed to fly. However, here we are in the next century, and it feels as though we have won a battle and lost a war. The importance of early childhood is being acknowledged worldwide. We have several revisions of the Early Years Foundation Stage (EYFS) framework, nursery grant entitlement for 2- and 3-year-olds in the UK and required qualifications for early years' practitioners. Yet large numbers of children and young people are illiterate and there is a growing concern regarding poor behaviour, culminating in a statement from Ofsted in 2014 that a vast amount of time in schools is wasted due to a culture of casual acceptance of bad behaviour. If early childhood education is in good shape, why is it that in 2015–2016 there were 3,035 fixed-term exclusions and 50 permanent exclusions issued to children aged 4 years or younger in state funded schools in England? Why are almost one in four children and young people showing some evidence of mental ill health including anxiety and depression (ONS, 2016) and, according to estimates from Public Health England (2017), two thirds of adults and a quarter of children between 2 and 10 years of age are overweight or obese? The report of Her Majesty's Chief Inspector of Education, Children's Services and Skills (Ofsted,

2015) concluded that although it was encouraging that outcomes for children from disadvantaged backgrounds are rising in line with their peers, there is no sign of the gap narrowing in any substantial way. Instead of getting off to a flying start, too many children are still falling into a gap of underachievement and poor outcomes.

This chapter explores lessons that we can learn from the past, including a review of the Start Right Report (Ball, 1994), Evidence from the Effective Pre-school and Primary Education Project (Sylva et al., 2010) and the implementation of the Early Years Foundation Stage (EYFS). The ground-breaking work conducted by many educators in order to convince politicians and the world of the importance of early childhood education is acknowledged. However, it is now time to take into consideration recent research and changes in society including the technology revolution. 'Tweaking' the current EYFS is not sufficient. It is time to re-define early childhood education and to replace the EYFS with a coherent curriculum from 0 to 7, taking into account stages of child development, the latest research and a world that has become international and made smaller by travel and technology.

Lessons from the past

When re-defining early childhood education, it is important to consider how our roots and personal experiences may be impacting our beliefs and values.

The first nursery school in the UK was established in Scotland by Robert Owen when he purchased four textile factories in 1810. You may be forgiven for imagining rows of desks and strict Victorian discipline. However, Owen was a philanthropist, believing that the right environment would produce good people. Part of Owen's vision was to build a school that included provision for nursery and infants as well as secondary education for children working in his factories. Formal education did not begin until children were 6 years old. Children spent their time roaming freely and learning singing and dancing from a variety of countries. Staff were required to develop loving and kind relationships with no physical punishments or harsh words. Owen instinctively had a deep understanding of the roots children needed. Surely this approach would provide a sound basis for education going forward?

Sadly, Owen's vision of education was not embraced by the politicians. Publicly funded education was introduced under the Forster Education Act of 1870, not as a result of a vision developed by those such as Owen, but prompted by a strong lobby from industrialists who believed that mass education was needed to maintain their manufacturing lead. Those concerned that the 1870 Act did not stop child labour were pleased when a further Act was passed in 1880 making attendance at school compulsory for children between the ages of 5 and 10. There was no educational rationale behind the starting age being 5. This starting point seems to have been 'plucked out of thin air', and not really thought about in the haste to get the legislation passed. Although there were some notable exceptions such as the open-air nursery for poor children opened by Margaret McMillan and her sister Rachel in 1911, the curriculum firmly consisted of reading, writing, arithmetic and non-denominational religious education. Pedagogy was characterised by rote learning and strict discipline, including the use of the cane and wearing of a dunce's cap for any children who were not able to learn. This polarisation of values, beliefs and methods has cast a shadow over early childhood education that persists to this day. There are still arguments about child-centred learning and the importance of a basic curriculum, direct teaching and discipline.

During the 1960s the Ministry of Education stated in Circular 8/60 that there was to be no expansion of nursery school provision. Out of this gap emerged the playgroup movement set up by Belle Tutaev, a young London mother who had started her own group when her daughter was unable to get a nursery place. There was also the growth of day care centres for working parents. This lack of commitment to nursery education sent a strong and lasting message that this stage of education was not important.

As time moved on, primary schools became the main providers of education for young children. The Plowden Report (1967) was a major milestone echoing the philosophy of Froebel that play is the main means of learning in early childhood with an integrated, holistic early childhood curriculum rather than individual subjects. The image of the teacher was portrayed as one of a *child grower* (Peters, 1969) who enables children to learn through discovery and to move on when they are ready. Bruce (1987) declared boldly that the rigid subject-divided curriculum had been rejected in favour of bringing everything together that the child learns through play. Although there was excitement about this approach there were also caveats. For example, Sylva, Roy and Painter (1980) reported that although the nursery teachers being observed were kind to the children, they were not very demanding and conversation between adult and child was limited with children not persisting at tasks. Meadows and Cashdan (1988) argued strongly that a high level of adult–child interaction was required during play in order to optimise children's learning.

By the early 1970s the arguments for nursery education were beginning to be heard, and in 1972 Margaret Thatcher, as Secretary of State for Education, presented the white paper 'A Framework for Expansion' (DES, 1972) in which it was proposed that nursery education be provided for all who wanted it, and that by 1980 there would be nursery school places for 50 per cent of 3-year-olds and 90 per cent of 4-year-olds.

This was the point at which I began training as a teacher. The philosophies of Dewey (1959) and Montessori (1972) strongly underpinned my, and my fellow students', training. We absorbed values that emphasised children's individuality and their right to choose rather than the teacher imposing a restrictive curriculum. We nodded as we learnt about Montessori's belief that the child is innately curious and intrinsically motivated, learning by doing and through play in an exciting indoor and outdoor environment. Although we learnt about Piaget's (1952 [1936]) clinical and observational studies describing children passing through an ordered sequence of development, including the sensorimotor stage (0–2 years) and pre-operational stage (2–7 years), and needing to be 'ready' before they moved on to the next stage, we also learnt about Vygotsky (1978) and the concept of the zone of proximal development whereby the adult is able to raise attainment by interacting with and supporting the learner. Less attention was paid to researchers such as Donaldson (1978) who challenged the idea of 'readiness', stating that this often led to a lack of structure in the curriculum and lack of progression.

The ensuing economic recession prevented the promised expansion of nursery places, although some local authorities attached nurseries to schools with part-time provision for 3-year-olds and full-time provision in Reception classes. Many parents still relied upon their own resources for early years provision, with membership of the Pre-school Playgroups association growing to 17,000. The economic downturn led to questions about the effectiveness of education and the training of a workforce able to meet the demands of the economy and the modern world. In 1976 the Labour Prime Minister, James Callaghan, made his famous Ruskin speech in which he referred to the curriculum as a *secret garden* posing a question mark over the effectiveness of modern teaching methods.

After teaching for over 10 years with the main guidance coming from my local authority, we were shaken-up in 1988 by the introduction of the National Curriculum and demands for accountability. Although the arguments were put forward for a balanced curriculum, the primary rationale for the change was to raise standards by making schools accountable for the outcomes of their pupils. Although the National Curriculum applied to children of compulsory school age (the term after a child's fifth birthday) there were also demands for children to be 'ready' to start school combined with the idea that maybe nursery education could help raise standards from the 'bottom'.

In 1989, Kenneth Baker (Education Secretary) asked Angela Rumbold (minister in the DES) to chair a Committee of Inquiry on the quality of the educational experience offered to 3- and 4-year olds. The Rumbold Report was submitted in 1990 to John MacGregor who had become secretary of state for education in July 1989. The report clearly stated that nursery education needed to be expanded to meet demand and that the quality of a good deal of existing provision also needed to be raised. It highlighted that for under-fives the process of education is as important as its content. Reflecting the earlier publication, *The Curriculum from 5 to 16* (DES, 1985), it recommended eight main areas of learning:

- aesthetic and creative;
- human and social;
- language and literacy;
- mathematics;
- physical;
- science;
- spiritual and moral;
- technology.

When I became a headteacher in the Solihull local authority during the 1990s the school, along with many others in the Borough, had a part-time nursery for

3-year-olds and full-time education for 4-year-olds in Reception classes. This arrangement was not consistent across the country, and there were many times that I defended the school having a nursery when colleagues accused us of diverting much needed funds from older children. Although we acknowledged the good work of playgroups, it is only upon reflection that I feel we did not express sufficiently our gratitude for the strong message that they gave to government with regard to the importance of early learning and the critical role of parents.

Although the Rumbold Report acknowledged the importance of early years education, it was the Start Right Report written by Sir Christopher Ball, Director of Learning for the Royal Society for the encouragement of Arts, Manufacturers and Commerce (RSA) that gave the following strong, uncompromising message:

> The current situation is little short of a national scandal. We have neglected the needs of the most vulnerable members of society – young children (especially those from deprived or disadvantaged backgrounds). Since 1972 governments of both left and right have failed to implement Margaret Thatcher's promise. For nearly a generation large numbers of the nation's children have been deprived of the right to start their lives, and society has paid the price in terms of educational failure and waste, low skills, disaffection and delinquency.
>
> The UK can (and should) ensure that 'no child born after the year 2000 be deprived of opportunity and support for effective early learning. Resources can be found. What has been lacking up to now is the political will'.
>
> *(Ball, 1994, p. 7)*

The Start Right Report of 1994 finally gave early childhood education the attention needed with five hard-hitting conclusions.

- Children's early learning, typically associated with the years three to six, forms a distinct and fundamental phase of education....It has its own proper curriculum – which is distinct from, and preparatory to Key Stage 1 of the National Curriculum.
- Parents, professionals and the community must work together in partnership since no one of them can be fully effective on their own.
- The following ten features of good practice should be systematically applied and guaranteed:
  - provision of many and varied opportunities for children and adults to talk and communicate about learning;
  - learning activities which are concrete, real and relevant to the lives of young children;
  - educators who acknowledge and utilise purposeful play as a powerful medium for learning;
  - adults who support and develop each child's self-esteem and identity, involve themselves in learning activities and extend children's learning by

asking and answering questions, and by stimulating the child's curiosity, imagination and wonder;

- opportunities for children to choose from a variety of activities, materials and equipment;
- provision for large groups, small groups, individual and solitary activities;
- outdoor experiences on a daily basis;
- periods of uninterrupted time to enable children to explore and engage in activities according to individual need and involvement;
- a balance of movement and rest in the daily programme;
- an achieved aim of ensuring that learning is fun.

(Ball, 1994 p. 55)

- It is possible for the UK to provide effective early learning – what had been lacking was the political will to do so.
- Action must be taken as the situation in 1994 is *little short of a national scandal* with large numbers of children being deprived of the right start to their lives resulting in *educational failure and waste, low skills, disaffection and delinquency.*

(Ball, 1994, p. 75)

The arguments were particularly powerful as they were underpinned by a comprehensive and critical review of research evidence linking high-quality care and education to lasting cognitive and social benefits in children, which led to The Effective Provision of Pre-School Education (EPPE Project) headed by Professor Kathy Sylva (Sylva et al., 2010). In appendix C of the Start Right Report, Kathy Sylva acknowledges the difficulties of countering arguments based upon early research that appeared to show the impact of pre-school experiences *washed out* soon after starting school. However, she highlights that most of the studies did not control adequately for pre-intervention differences in ability and few used comparison groups. Having presented the weaknesses of such analyses, she goes on to present further research evidence, including the Perry Pre-school project, later known as the High/scope research that strongly links quality pre-school experiences to positive outcomes for children. A key finding that is just as relevant today is that, although an initial IQ advantage for those who participated in the programme disappeared by secondary school, the long-term impact on the children's personal and social development and outcomes were striking. For example, a significantly higher number of the programme children completed high school – 71 per cent compared with 54 per cent and there were significantly fewer arrests by age 27–7 per cent compared with 35 per cent.

A cross-departmental review of services for young children was instigated, concluding that disadvantage among young children was increasing, with un-coordinated and patchy services. From this emerged the introduction of the Sure Start project in 1998. Sure Start aimed to provide children with the best possible start in life through improved childcare, early education, health and family support. There was an emphasis on outreach and community development focusing on the 20 per cent most deprived areas, which included about half of families with incomes below the official poverty line. The Government allocated £452 million between 1998 and 2002 to create 250 local programmes reaching 150,000 children in areas of deprivation.

The Effective Provision of Pre-School Education (EPPE Project) led by Professor Kathy Sylva, begun in 1997, underpinned the Government's promise to prioritise early childhood provision. This unique comprehensive longitudinal study focused on the effects of different kinds of pre-school provision and the factors that affected young children's progress and attainment. The EPPE research examined a group of 2,800 children drawn from randomly selected pre-school settings in England and a group of 200 *home children* who had no pre-school experience.

The initial findings were published in 2003 and the study was extended to follow the cohort to just beyond their GCSE Year (2013). With regard to Early Years, the report found that:

- Pre-school experience enhances children's development.
- An earlier start is related to better intellectual development and improved independence, concentration and sociability.
- Full-time attendance did not provide better gains compared with part-time attendance.
- Disadvantaged children particularly benefit from good quality pre-school experiences, especially if they attend centres that cater for different social backgrounds.
- Good quality can be found across all types of early years settings, but overall higher quality was found in integrated settings, nursery schools and nursery classes.
- Settings were of a higher quality and children made more progress where there were staff with higher qualifications including a good proportion of qualified teachers.
- Children made better all-round progress in settings where educational and social development were of equal importance.
- Effective pedagogy included the provision of *instructive learning environments* and *sustained shared thinking* to extend children's learning.

Kathy Sylva (Ball, 1994, p. 104) defined curriculum as the *concepts, knowledge, understanding, attitudes and skills that we wish children to develop*. She highlighted the key principles that underpin the education of all children; that to promote the spiritual, moral, cultural and mental development of children, the curriculum needs to be broad, balanced, differentiated and relevant, and to take into account the assessment of children's progress, equal opportunities and special educational needs. As a result, children will be prepared for the opportunities, responsibilities and experiences of adult life.

A significant step towards a framework encompassing the findings of the EPPE research was the publication of the *Desirable Outcomes for Children's Learning* (DfEE,

1996). In Spring 1999, the Qualifications and Curriculum Authority (QCA) consulted widely prior to the announcement of a distinct *Foundation Stage* for children aged 3 to the end of the reception year. *Curriculum Guidance for the Foundation Stage* was published in 2000 by the QCA, and Nick Tate, CEO of the QCA stated in the foreword: 'The establishment of a foundation stage is a significant landmark in funded education in England. For the first time it gives this very important stage of education a distinct identity.'

In 2002 the DfES published *Birth to Three Matters* based on the stages of child development rather than the areas of learning. The amalgamation of these documents into a single framework in 2007 was a positive step towards coherent provision for early childhood education even though some were concerned that curriculum pressures would filter down to those providing for the very young. The Tickell review (DfE 2011a, 2011b) confirmed that there should continue to be a framework that applies to all providers working with children in the early years. However, a recommendation to allow exemptions for the learning and development requirements for independent schools and for settings governed by established principles such the Steiner Waldorf schools was implemented. This enabled Steiner Waldorf settings to continue with their established principle that children are not taught to read and write before rising 7. Key recommendations to make communication and language and physical development identified as prime areas of learning and to reduce the early learning goals from 69 to 17 with a scale to assess whether children were *emerging, expected or exceeding* were also implemented. Although the disconnect from the EYFS to Key Stage 1 was acknowledged, the emphasis was placed upon Reception teachers preparing children for Year One and the National Curriculum rather than seeing the early childhood phase extending to age 6/7 as recommended in the Start Right Report (1994).

The DfE commissioned the Evaluation of Children's Centres in England (ECCE) to provide an in-depth understanding of the effects of different approaches in the management and delivery of children's centre services between 2009 and 2015. The report (Sammons et al., 2015) found that there were mixed findings from Phase One, suggesting that although 86 per cent of the sample were achieving some positive outcomes, a smaller group of the most disadvantaged families, particularly teen mothers, were doing less well than their peers in non-Sure Start areas. The Phase Two findings with a sample of over 9, 000 found that at age 3 children in the Sure Start areas:

- demonstrated better social and emotional development;
- had fewer accidental injuries with a higher likelihood of receiving all recommended immunisations;
- demonstrated no statistically significant effects on children's verbal ability as measured by the British Ability Scales (BAS) Naming Vocabulary, and no reduction in negative social behaviour.

It was also found that there were no effects of living in a Sure Start area on children's development in terms of the Foundation Stage Profile ratings; no effects on child social and emotional development and no effect on whether or not a child had one or more accidents since 9 months of age.

Over 5,000 children in Start Right areas were assessed at age 7 using assessments for Key Stage 1 in reading, writing, maths and science, social and emotional outcomes, which considered emotional dysregulation, positive social behaviour, internalisation and self-regulation and health outcomes. There was again no consistent effect of Sure Start centres when compared with children in non-Sure Start areas.

The report concluded that children centre services have the potential to improve the effects of disadvantage, promoting better parenting, health and social skills, but the centres cannot on their own overcome the adverse effects of being part of a disadvantaged family living in a disadvantaged neighbourhood. Following this conclusion, the government suspended Ofsted inspections of children's centres in 2015. Rather than consider what needed to be added to the Sure Start programme since 2010 the government has announced the closure of 350 Sure Start Centres and is considering the future direction for those remaining. Reduced funding has also changed the way the remaining centres operate, with an increase in multiple sites, the delivery of targeted programmes and a reduction in open access.

The revised EYFS framework of 2017 fails to take into account the latest research and changes to our society. As with previous iterations of the EYFS, it has continued to perpetuate a cut-off point at the end of the Reception Year instead of providing a coherent stage from 0 to 7. The Recent Ofsted Report *Bold Beginnings* (2017, p. 4) states

> Reception and Year 1 teachers agreed that the vital, smooth transition from the foundation stage to Year 1 was difficult because the early learning goals were not aligned with the now-increased expectations of the national curriculum. Progression and continuity in mathematics were seen as particularly problematic.
>
> Put simply, by the end of Reception, the ability to read, write and use numbers is fundamental. They are the building blocks for all other learning. Without firm foundations in these areas, a child's life chances can be severely restricted. The basics need to be taught – and learned – well, from the start.
>
> *(Ofsted, 2017 p. 10)*

I believe weaknesses in the reliability and validity of the Early Years Foundations Stage Profile (EYFSP) are masking underachievement and are at the root of a divide between Reception and Year One. Early Years practitioners spend a great deal of time assessing children against the early learning goals with local authorities moderating and producing statistics that indicate things are improving. In 2013, 52 per cent of children reached a 'good' level of development. By 2017 this had risen to 71 per cent. In 2017, the percentage of children achieving at least the expected level within the 17 early learning goals ranged between 80 and 90 per cent. The research described in Chapter 4 highlights that most children in the research project began the Reception Year below the norms for physical development despite

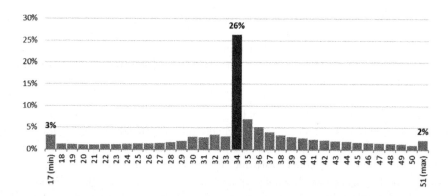

FIGURE 2.1 Total points score distribution in the EYFSP for all pupils. England, 2017

Source: DfE 2017, p. 4.

having achieved or exceeded the early learning goal for physical development. Furthermore, analysis of the distribution of total points scored shows a distinctive spike at 34 points – the equivalent of a child achieving the expected level of development (see Figure 2.1).

Clark (2014) found a similar pattern when she analysed the results of the phonics test administered to all children in state schools in Year One. There was an increase in pupils passing the test from 58 per cent in 2012, to 69 per cent in 2013 and 74 per cent in 2014, with 88 per cent of pupils meeting the expected standard by the end of Year Two. Following regression analysis, Clark suggests that the spike at the threshold of meeting the expected standard indicates that pupils on the borderline may have been marked up. I believe that this also applies to the EYFSP.

Amanda Spielman, upon her recent appointment as the Ofsted Chief Inspector of Schools has made public that schools should focus on providing a well-rounded education that concentrates on the curriculum and substance of education. This is a distinct and welcome change in tone. However, in order to bring about this change we need to re-define early childhood education and implement a curriculum and pedagogy that works. I suggest that this requires the following steps:

1   Replace the EYFS with Key Stage 1 covering 0 to 7 years (Kindergarten: 0 to 2 years; Nursery: 2 to 3 years; Reception: 4 to 5 years; Year One: 5 to 6 years; Year Two: 6 to 7 years). This will enable progression to Key Stage 2 and integration into later key stages.

2   Embrace the principles of early childhood education first iterated in the Start Right Report of 1994.

3   Stop the EYFSP: combine teacher/practitioner assessment with a standardised assessment against national norms in language, mathematics and physical development.

4   Update the curriculum for early learning originally developed by Professor Kathy Sylva (Ball, 1994, p. 104).
5   Provide early years teachers/practitioners with training/qualifications in providing courses and support for parents in effective parenting and parental engagement.

It is time to move away from the old arguments that standardised testing is at the expense of child-centred education, early childhood core principles including learning through play, and teacher assessment. I was part of the team that developed the University of Durham CEM Centre Performance Indicators in Primary Schools (PIPS) baseline in the 1990s. These tests do not purport to replace teacher assessment but to add to it with valid and reliable data against national norms. Following the research conducted on the physical development of Reception age children described in Chapter 4 of this book, I am delighted that CEM is now going to include tests of physical development in the baseline. Rather than waste time and money on unreliable testing and expending energy on trying to raise the school starting age, let us begin the process of re-defining early childhood education with the independent sector and schools disapplied from the EYFS learning and development requirements. Already others are seizing the initiative. For example, Dr Kay Sanderson and I are working with the Ministry in the UAE to implement the approaches suggested in this book.

In the final section of this chapter I present a new curriculum framework that I have devised for the Key Stage 1 (birth to 7 years of age). It re-defines the areas of learning, advocating a pedagogy that is multi-sensory, active and play-based.

A Framework for the Future

The following proposed Early Years curriculum framework is designed to provide the school or setting with a structure to plan activities and experiences taking into account the developmental stage and interests of the child. This includes *in the moment planning* as described in Chapter 8, where the teacher follows the interests and learning of the child, providing opportunities and extension based on continuous observation. Formative assessment based on observation is used to plan the next steps of learning combined with a two-year check, tests of vision and hearing at the start of school and standardised tests in literacy, numeracy and physical development at the start and end of Reception, end of Year One and end of Year Two. As with the Scandinavian model, formative assessments are shared with parents but are not submitted to government for data analysis. During inspections, inspectors will be able to judge the quality of formative assessment as well as outcomes measured by standardised tests.

Physical development is given particular emphasis in order to provide children with the sensory, gross and fine motor movements that they need for learning. World languages and cultural understanding have been combined with communication as it is now time to build upon our knowledge of how babies and young children learn language. The baby makes the sound of every language in the world. He or she filters out the unwanted sounds as language is absorbed from those around him or her. The vocal chords also begin to 'harden off' from age 3 making it difficult to produce sounds outside of the range that is in use. Our diverse communities give us a wide range of opportunities to introduce our children to a variety of languages from native speakers through music, story and song. By opening our children's systems to language learning with an oral and active approach we truly begin to give our children an understanding of the world.

Technology has revolutionised the world and the way that we communicate. However, Sigman (2017) presents research linking screen use to delays in oral language development and later tendencies towards addiction. In a study of 248 healthy children aged 5–17 years, increased video game play was associated with unfavourable neurocognitive development reported in line with those implicated in studies of gambling disorders and substance addiction. In a study of 894 children between ages 6 months and 2 years from 2011 to 2015, researchers found that the more handheld screen time a child's parent reported, the more likely the child was to have delays in expressive speech. For each 30-minute increase in handheld screen time, researchers found a 49 per cent increased risk of expressive speech delay (Birken, 2017). These results support a recent policy recommendation by the American Academy of Paediatrics to discourage any type of screen media in children younger than 18 months. These findings have been taken into account when planning the digital learning strand below.

The original curriculum developed by Kathy Sylva referred to science and to history and geography. Wrapping these into *Understanding the World* has created confusion and has in my opinion, watered-down these areas of learning. I have therefore re-instated these areas as well as adding digital learning as a separate strand.

In my view, it is not possible to identify *prime areas of learning*, as for the young child all learning is integrated and connected enabling them to develop the executive functions of working memory, inhibition and cognitive flexibility described by Karen Morris in Chapter 7. I propose that teachers and practitioners responsible for children from birth to 7 years use the following framework as a basis for planning.

TABLE 2.1 Revised Early Years Curriculum Framework. Preedy (2018)

Health, Safety, Personal, Social and Emotional Development	Provide opportunities for children to form strong attachments with key person(s).
	Support children in appreciating what makes them unique including name, birthday, family, gender, appearance, culture and language.
	Nurture and motivate children in order that they can think positively, develop high self-esteem, self-confidence, flexibility, resilience and happiness.
	Support children in caring for and helping others; enabling children to reflect and understand their feelings and to manage their behaviour appropriately including understanding rules and the development of negotiation and conflict-resolution skills.

(Continued)

TABLE 2.1 (Continued)

	Enable children to independently think, seek challenges, make connections, make choices, be resourceful, ask questions, take risks, persevere and overcome failure in order to achieve mastery of their learning.
	Enable children to interact positively with others including role play, collaboration, turn-taking and sharing.
	Enable children to manage change and transitions including transition to their next class or stage of education.
	Support children in understanding the principles of nutrition through cooking, trying a variety of food and drink and eating a balanced diet.
	Support children in understanding the link between exercise, diet, sufficient sleep and being healthy.
	Support children in understanding how to be safe; enable them to manage their own personal hygiene including going to the toilet, washing hands, combing hair and brushing teeth.
Physical Development	Test children's vision and hearing at age 4/5 years (intervention as appropriate).
	Enable children to explore, respond to and process sound through dance and a variety of songs, rhymes, music and instrumental experiences.
	Build movement and multi-sensory opportunities into all aspects of learning enabling children to develop control, balance, an awareness of space, co-ordination, fine and gross motor skills.
	Provide children with daily opportunities for outside play including riding bikes and trikes, running, jumping, skipping and being active for continuous periods of time.
Communication, World Languages, Citizenship and Universal Understanding	Support children in using and responding to eye contact and a range of body movements and facial expressions.
	Enable children to listen, follow instructions and to express themselves confidently using a range of vocabulary and structures during role play and in a variety of situations.
	Enable children to link sounds, symbols and letters in order to read and write confidently at least in line with expectations for their age group.
	Provide opportunities for children to enjoy fiction and non-fiction books, poetry, drama and stories, and to be able to draw upon these to develop their literacy skills.

TABLE 2.1 (Continued)

	Provide opportunities for children to learn about their country of residence, its roots, laws and values; experience a wide range of languages and cultures including languages spoken by children for whom English is an Additional language; provide opportunities for children to become confident in at least two languages.
Mathematical Development	Provide practical opportunities for matching, comparing, ordering, sorting, counting and understanding numbers including more than and less than, doubling and halving; calculating, problem-solving and reasoning using addition, subtraction, multiplication and division; shape, space and measure; time; money; mathematical patterns.
Scientific Development	Provide opportunities for children to find out about living things (humans, animals, insects and plants); rocks and soil, forces, solids and liquids, materials, electricity, the weather, earth and space. Support children in being able to observe closely; predict, ask questions, draw conclusions and independently record their findings.
History and Geography	Develop a sense of place. Learn about change and the history of their family, school and location. Learn about people now and in the past. Be able to locate countries and features on a globe and a map. Understand weather, seasons and how climates vary in different parts of the world. Consider how climate impacts people, animals and plants. Take action to care for their environment and the wider world.
Digital Learning	Support children in using a range of programmable toys. Enable children to use technology to communicate with children around the world. Enable children to gather safely information from different sources and to use technology to support learning across the curriculum. *No screentime for the under twos. No more than an hour a day for children aged 2 to 5. No more than 15 minutes at a time.* *Ensure that children can actually see Interactive Whiteboards and that their visual processing is not distorted by distance or angle – including looking upward from the floor. No more than 15 minutes at a time watching the screen.*

TABLE 2.1 (Continued)

Creativity, Art and Design	Provide children with a wide range of materials and tools in order to develop their creative and manipulative skills including cutting, drawing, painting gluing, sticking, printing, sculpting and weaving and sewing.
	Provide opportunities to use construction toys and junk materials to create 3-dimensial structures.
	Incorporate creative opportunities across all areas of learning.
Early Intervention for additional needs including second language learning	Test children's vision and hearing to ensure these are within the *normal* range.
	Use formative and standardised assessments to identify children who are giving cause for concern/performing below their chronological age or ability in physical development, numeracy or literacy (taking into account whether the language of instruction is not in the child's first language(s).
	Put in place individual education plans with specific interventions to meet the additional needs of identified children.
	Engage the services of appropriate professionals such as speech and language therapists and occupational therapists.
Extension for when children demonstrate ability and talent	Continually extend children's language, thought and learning across all areas of the curriculum by providing a wide range of challenges that can be tackled independently and collaboratively.
	Provide children with inspiring examples, role models and, where appropriate, external input and coaching from experts.

The latest version of the *EYFS Statutory Framework* (DfE, 2017a, 2017b) effectively details the requirements for child protection and keeping children safe, including the appointment of suitable people. When discussing adult-to-child ratios with Sir Christopher, he referred to the *RSA rule of thumb* where you simply took the age of the child and doubled it to calculate the ratio of staff required. For example, if a child was aged five, the ratio would be one adult to ten children. This simple formula enables funding to be shifted to younger children as the ratio for older students would become higher, e.g. at university ratios would be in the region of 1 to 40. Taking this formula into account, I propose the following adult to child ratios and minimum qualification requirements. These build upon current UK practice but continue through to the end of our definition of Key Stage 1. It will of course be necessary to increase grant funding in order that all schools and settings can afford to employ quality staff throughout the early childhood stage.

The following chapters of this book bring life to the proposed curriculum framework, highlighting research, strategies and interventions that have made a difference to outcomes for young children. In Chapter 3 Sally Goddard Blythe explains the connection between movement and learning. In Chapter 4 Rebecca

TABLE 2.2 Adult to child ratios and minimum qualification requirements

Age	Adult to child ratio	Minimum qualification requirements
Under 2	1:3	Level 3 for all practitioners.
2 +	1:4	Level 3 for all practitioners.
3 +	1:8	Early Years Teacher for the leader of this year group + Level 3 Assistants.
4 + (Reception)	1:10	Early Years Teacher per class + Level 3 Assistants.
5 + (Year One)	1:10	Teacher per class (must have relevant EY training and or experience) + Level 3 Assistants.
6 + (Year Two)	1:15	Teacher per class (must have relevant EY training and or experience) + Level 3 Assistant.

Duncombe and I share our *Movement for Learning* research, indicating that inactivity may be contributing to poor physical and sensory development and the positive impact of introducing a daily movement programme in the Reception year. Chapters 5 and 6 focus upon parenting. Kay Sanderson, Rosie Hamilton McGinty and I share research that enables parents to engage with their children – an area that Sir Christopher highlights as still very much needed in our modern world. In Chapter 7 Karen Morris explores the importance of the executive functions of working memory, inhibition and attention to early learning. In Chapter 8 Samantha Steed provides a case study demonstrating how to create a play-based environment that enhances rather than compromises standards. My belief in standardised tests underpinned by teacher assessment does not mean that creativity is squeezed out. In Chapter 9 Ruth Churchill Dower leads the way in highlighting how creative experiences impact brain and physical development, imagination, confidence, self-esteem and behaviour. Finally, in Chapter 10 Helen Wright sets the book within a global context, encouraging and challenging us to widen our perspective.

We need to give our children the wings they need to fly in today's world and in the future. Let us begin the process of re-defining early childhood education and getting it right from the start.

References

Ball, C. (1994). *Start Right: The importance of early learning*. London: RSA.

Birken, C. (2017). Is handheld screen time use associated with language delay in infants? 2017 Pediatric Academic Societies Meeting, San Francisco.

Bruce, T. (1987). *Early childhood education*. London: Hodder and Stoughton.

Callaghan, J. (1976). A relational debate based on the facts. Ruskin College, Oxford. 18 October, 1976. http://www.educationengland.org.uk/documents/speeches/1976ruskin.html

Carter, W. H. (1953). *Where Main Street meets the river*. New York: Rinehart and Company.

Clark, M. M. (2014). *Learning to be literate: Insights from research for policy and practice.* Birmingham: Glendale Education.

Department of Education and Science (DES). (1972). *White paper: Education: A framework for expansion.* London: HMSO.

Department of Education and Science (DES). (1985). *The curriculum from 5 to 16.* London: HMSO.

Dewey, J. (1959). *School and society.* Chicago: University of Chicago Press.

DfE. (2011a). *The Early Years: Foundations for life, health and learning. An independent report on the Early Years Foundation Stage to Her Majesty's government.* London: DfE.

DfE. (2011b). *The Early Years Foundation Stage (EYFS) review report on the evidence.* London: DfE.

DfE. (2017a). *The Early Years Foundation Stage (EYFS) learning and development requirements: Guidance on exemptions for early years providers.* London: DfE.

DfE. (2017b). *Statutory framework for the early years foundation stage. Setting the standards for learning, development and care for children from birth to five.* London: DfE.

DfEE. (1996). *Desirable outcomes for children's learning on entering compulsory education.* London: DfEE.

DfES. (2002). *Birth to Three Matters.* London: DfES.

Donaldson, M. (1978). *Children's minds.* Glasgow: Fontana/Collins.

Meadows, S., & Cashdan, A. (1988). *Helping children learn.* London. David Fulton.

Montessori, M. (1972). *Dr. Montessori's own handbook: A short guide to her ideas and materials.* New York: Schocken Books.

Ofsted (2014). *Below the radar: Low-level disruption in the country's classrooms.* London: Ofsted.

Ofsted (2015). *The annual report of Her Majesty's Chief Inspector of education, children's services and skills 2015/16.* London: Ofsted.

Ofsted (2017). *Bold beginnings: The Reception curriculum in a sample of good and outstanding primary schools.* London: Ofsted.

ONS. (2016). *Selected children's well-being measures by country.* London: ONS.

Peters, R. (Ed.). (1969). *Perspectives on Plowden.* London: Routledge & Kegan Paul.

Piaget, J. (1952 [1936]). *The origins of intelligence in children.* Trans. M. Cook. Madison, CT: International Universities Press.

Plowden Report. (1967). *Children and their primary schools. A report of the Central Advisory Council for Education (England).* London: HMSO.

Public Health England (2017). Health matters: Obesity and the food environment. https://www.gov.uk/government/publications/health-matters-obesity-and-the-food-environment/health-matters-obesity-and-the-food-environment—2

Qualifications and Curriculum Authority (QCA). (1999). *Early learning goals. Pre-School period.* London: QCA.

Qualifications and Curriculum Authority (QCA). (2000). *Curriculum guidance for the Foundation Stage.* London: SCAA.

Rumbold Report. (1990). *Starting with quality. The report of the Committee of Inquiry into the quality of the educational experience offered to 3- and 4-year-olds, chaired by Mrs Angela Rumbold CBE, MP.* London: HMSO.

Sammons, P., Hall, J., Smees, R., Goff, G., Sylva, K., Smith, T., Evangelou, E., Eisenstadt, N., & Smith, G. (2015). *The impact of children's centres: studying the effects of children's centres in promoting better outcomes for young children and their families evaluation of children's centres in England (ECCE, strand 4) technical appendices.* University of Oxford.

Sigman, A. (2017). *Screen Dependency Disorders: a new challenge for child neurology.* JICNA. ISSN 2410–6410. Available at: http://jicna.org/index.php/journal/article/view/67

Sylva, K., Melhuish, E., Sammons, P., Siraj-Blatchford, I., & Taggart, B. (2010). *Early childhood matters: Evidence from the effective pre-school and primary education project* Oxon: Routledge.

Sylva, K., Roy, C., & Painter. M. (1980). *Childwatching at playgroup and nursery school. Vol. 2. Oxford preschool research project*. Michigan: High/Scope Press.

Vygotsky, L. S. (1978). *Mind in society: The development of higher psychological processes*. Cambridge, MA: Harvard University Press.

3

MOVEMENT A CHILD'S FIRST A, B, C

Sally Goddard Blythe

We now know so much more about the brain and how movement and the senses are linked to children's development and learning. However, the *application* of this knowledge is years behind, as educational policy tends to focus on *outcomes*, opting to turn a Nelsonian 'blind eye' to the *processes* of how children learn.

This chapter highlights the work of INPP (Institute of Neuro-Physiological Psychology) and explores recent research and the development of our knowledge and understanding of the relationship between children's physical abilities and learning.

The importance of the development of balance, sensory development and integration is explained, as well as how movement experience is involved in the integration of early reflexes, which support posture, balance and coordination throughout life.

In our modern world children are moving less and this is impacting their development, readiness for school and performance. This chapter underpins the theory behind the *Movement for Learning Project* described in Chapter 4 and explores other projects which have taken The INPP Movement Programme into schools for use with older children (Year 2 upwards).

Understanding the link between movement and learning

The time of greatest brain development is during the early years. Lack of stimulation and limited movement opportunities can have a lasting effect on a child's development and learning. In order to understand the link between movement and learning it is important to understand how physical development supports aspects of cognitive learning.

Balance

Balance, sometimes described as 'the forgotten sense' because it has no special sensation of its own, is essential for functioning in a gravity-based environment.

Balance is not something we have, it is something we *do*, and is the product of several systems operating together. Balance is as an internal sensory system that provides the basis for stability in space and which only reaches conscious awareness when it is challenged in some way. When disturbed, it affects levels of arousal, heightens sensation experienced through other senses and can result in perceptual disturbances.

We have all experienced instances when the sense of balance is taken outside its comfort zone: Rollercoasters for example directly stimulate the balance mechanism by making rapid and sudden stomach churning changes of direction and speed; motion sickness – sometimes described as the balance mechanism's 'special form of sickness' – occurs when the normal functional relationship between the vestibular system (*balance mechanism located in the inner ear*), vision and proprioception (*sense of perception, usually at the subconscious level of the movements and position of the body; this sense is gained primarily from input from sensory nerve terminals in muscles and tendons (muscle spindles) and the fibrous capsule of joints combined with input from the vestibular apparatus*) is disturbed as a result of a specific type of motion: Sitting on a train in a railway station, if the train alongside pulls out of the station, the brain may be temporarily fooled into thinking it is our train that is moving (visual stimulus); if we spin rapidly, for a few seconds after the spinning has stopped our visual world appears to move. Motion sickness is often preceded by a heightened sense of smell or taste. These are all examples of how stimulation of the vestibular or functionally related systems can alter stability, excitation, sensation and perception. How is this relevant to children in school?

The most advanced level of balance is the ability to stay totally still (Goddard Blythe, 2012). Children who have poor balance may appear clumsy, have a tendency to fall over, bump into things, be uncoordinated in the playground and struggle to be successful at sports. This can affect participation in group activities and peer relationships, and also make a child an easy target for bullying.

There is a difference between static and dynamic balance. Static balance refers to the ability to remain stationary and is necessary to sit still and carry out coordinated acts, while dynamic balance is the ability to maintain balance whilst in motion or when switching between positions. Good control of balance involves the ability to remain still or 'poised' between different phases of motion.

Learning to ride a bicycle provides a good example of the relationship between speed and balance. In the early stages, control of balance is achieved once in motion and wobble only starts to set in when slowing down to stop, start or change direction. In other words, speed or momentum can compensate for inadequate control of balance.

Children with poor control of static balance may appear reasonably well coordinated when running, on the sports field or moving in the playground but find it difficult to sit still in class. Paradoxically, if these children are allowed more opportunities to move around at regular intervals through the school day, their ability to sit still and pay attention in class tends to improve.

Balance is also important because it is linked through *postural control* to centres involved in the control of eye movements essential to support reading, writing, copying and catching a ball.

Postural control

Postural control is the product of an involuntary neurological loop consisting of motor, sensory and integrative processes used to maintain the body's position relative to gravity and of its segments relative to each other for stability. Balance is a hallmark of postural control.

Postural control and balance are inter-dependent and start to develop within weeks of birth. The human infant is born at a relatively immature stage of development compared with other mammals that are able to get up on to their feet and access feeding for themselves within minutes of being born. In contrast it takes the human infant 9–12 months to develop these skills, which will support mobility and independent learning for life. In biology, *altrical* species are those in which the young are incapable of moving around on their own soon after hatching or being born. The word is derived from the Latin root *alere* meaning to nurse, to rear, or to nourish indicating the need for young to be fed and taken care of for a long duration. Woven into this *altricial* period are two groups of reflexes, which support pre-motile and independent movement respectively.

Primitive reflexes

Primitive reflexes are stereotyped responses to specific stimuli. They emerge during life in the womb, are fully developed in a healthy full-term baby and are gradually inhibited in the first 6 months of post-natal life as connections to higher centres in the brain develop. Well recognised examples include the palmar grasp and suck reflexes (see Figures 3.1 and 3.2).

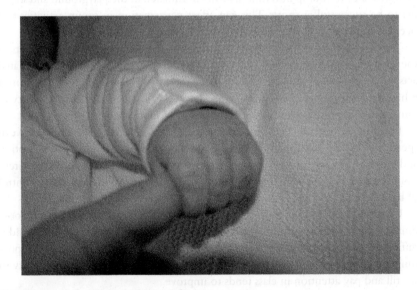

FIGURE 3.1   Infant grasp (palmar) reflex

Source: With permission of Hawthorn Press, Stroud. *Born to move. 2018.*

FIGURE 3.2   Infant sucking reflex

Source: With permission of Hawthorn Press, Stroud. *Born to move. 2018.*

Primitive reflexes are inhibited primarily through the process of maturation of the central nervous system (CNS), but this process is also linked to experience. It is affected if there is neurological impairment and is a recognised sign of Cerebral Palsy (CP) and other forms of brain injury, but in normal development it is enhanced and entrained through movement *experience*. If maturation is 'hard wired' into the healthy brain at birth, then experience is the environmental 'software' that builds the architecture of the developing brain.

Retention of primitive reflexes in children beyond the first year of life provides recognised signposts of immaturity in the functioning of the central nervous system. There is a continuum from which, at the severe end, retained primitive reflexes are accepted signs of pathology (CP being one example) but to a milder degree they can also feature in Developmental Coordination Disorder and learning-disabled children (Gustaffsson, 1971; Rider, 1976). Traces of infant reflexes have also been found in children with specific learning difficulties (Bender, 1976; McPhillips, Hepper & Mulhern, 2000) including attention deficit hyperactivity disorder (ADHD) (O'Dell & Cooke, 2004; Taylor, Houghton, & Chapman, 2004). The primitive reflexes are not necessarily the primary cause of related learning difficulties, rather they provide markers or indicators of immaturity in the functioning of the CNS that subsequently act as barriers to specific aspects of learning.

Postural reflexes (reactions)

Muscle tone and postural control develop rapidly in the first years of life. As primitive reflexes are inhibited in the first six months, they are gradually integrated/replaced or transformed into postural reactions, which collectively provide the basis for subconscious control of posture, balance and coordination.

Postural reactions support a child in becoming an active explorer in space who can roll, sit, crawl, stand, walk and run. They underpin an individual's response to a loss of balance and weight change in order to maintain body alignment or posture in space, and they also provide a stable platform for centres involved in the control of eye movements necessary for reading and writing, judging space and depth, being able to separate foreground from background (necessary to maintain eye contact) and adjust focus at speed between different visual distances.

Empirical evidence obtained from a doctor in the United States working with adolescents and college age students found that students who had managed to reach required standards at primary and secondary school, but who started to fail, drop out of college or experienced emotional problems such as depression after entering higher education, all showed similar profiles of under-developed postural reactions. It was his belief that postural reactions are essential to support higher aspects of learning and emotional self-regulation.

> The under-development or absence of postural reflexes has much greater influence on symptom development and functional limitations in this older population. Any deficiency in the critical systems of postural control must be compensated for by the intervention of the highest (most recently evolved) areas of the CNS. This follows Jackson's Law – the most highly developed, most complex functions will be sacrificed to maintain functions earlier evolved, more primitive, and more critical to survival. In humans these encompass high-level and complex cortical activities such as comprehension, executive function, analytical and synthetic abilities, as well as cognitive and processing competence.
>
> *(Beuret, 2017, pp. 280–291)*

In other words, postural reactions function rather like an efficient secretary to the executive parts of the brain. When the office management team is working efficiently the executive is free to concentrate on the higher functions of planning, processing, problem solving, adaptation and innovation.

Reflexes and learning

In 1975, PhD Psychologist Peter Blythe set up the Institute for Neuro-Physiological Psychology (INPP) with the aims of:

1   researching into physical foundations for learning and emotional regulation in children and adults;

2   developing reliable methods of assessing signs of immaturity in physical pro-
     cesses that underpin learning and emotional regulation;
3   developing effective remedial programmes.

Although the role of primitive and postural reflexes in development and their
diagnostic significance in pathology had long been recognised, Blythe and colleagues were the first to use the reflexes, not just as clinical tools for diagnosis, but
to identify which individual reflexes could be related to specific educational difficulties (Blythe & McGlowan, 1979), and to develop a unique physical intervention
programme, which used the reflexes as clinical 'maps' to indicate the developmental
level of movement needed to remediate the underlying problems and to measure
change during and after intervention.

The following review of some of the reflexes is based on their work. It helps
to illustrate the relationship between immature reflexes and learning outcomes.
It should be stressed that not all of the 'symptoms' listed as being associated with
retention of a reflex will be present in all cases.

The Moro reflex

The Moro reflex emerges from 9–12 weeks after conception and should be fully
developed in the healthy infant born at full term.

It is activated by a sudden change of position or other sensory stimuli with
the vestibular (balance) system being particularly sensitive in the early weeks
of life.

The arms extend outwards, there is a sharp intake of breath, a momentary
'freeze', followed by the return of the arms into a clasping position and exhalation,
usually accompanied by a sharp cry. It is an instantaneous reaction to sudden or
aversive stimuli from which the infant is unable to protect itself. It is a primitive
fight/flight reaction.

The Moro reflex is normally inhibited at circa 4 months of age, when it is
gradually replaced by a developing adult 'startle' reaction.

In contrast to the Moro reflex, which is an immediate reaction to perceived
threat, activated before conscious awareness, the startle reaction involves blinking in
response to the stimulus, use of the senses to search the environment to identify the
source of 'startle' and then either reaction to the stimulus if warranted, or disregard-
ing it. In other words, the more mature startle reaction involves a cortical (thinking)
decision, whereas the Moro reflex reacts first and thinks later.

While the Moro reflex is a natural reaction before an infant has the postural
control or motor coordination to defend or support itself, if it remains active in a
school-aged child it can be associated with the following:

•   tendency to over-react to minor stimuli;
•   tendency to be over-sensitive to specific stimuli;
•   hyper-vigilance;

FIGURE 3.3   The Moro reflex

Source: With permission of Wiley Blackwell. Chichester (Goddard Blythe, 2017).

- stimulus bound – inability to ignore peripheral sensory stimuli to maintain attention on one thing. This may be present in one or several sensory modalities resulting in a child who is easily distracted;
- anticipatory anxiety.

Children with a residual Moro reflex often present as being emotionally immature or labile with a negative impact on relationships.

The Asymmetrical Tonic Neck Reflex

Present at birth in the mature neonate, the Asymmetrical Tonic Neck Reflex (ATNR) is a response to rotation of the head to either side eliciting extension of the arm and leg on the face side and flexion of the limbs on the back of the head side (see Figure 3.4). The eyes also follow the movement and direction of the head.

The visual system of a new born is immature. A baby needs to learn how to use the eyes in combination with information from other senses to develop clear vision at different visual distances, adjustment between visual distances, conjugate eye movements and the basis for visual perception. The ATNR is thought to play a part in early training of this complex process.

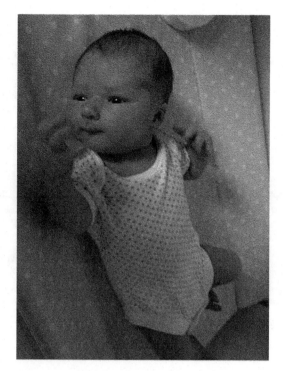

FIGURE 3.4   Asymmetrical Tonic Neck Reflex in new born

Source: With permission of Wiley Blackwell, Chichester.

The visual world of the new born is very different from what we later come to understand as vision in adulthood. The part of the brain that coordinates the muscles that move the eyes with the objects someone sees is immature, as is the fovea – the part of the eye on which objects are most sharply focused – focal distance in the first days of life is limited to 12–17 cm from the face and the eyes are drawn to outlines at the expense of central detail. An infant must literally learn how to see.

In the early weeks of life, when the ATNR is active, as the head to turns to one side, the head, the eyes and the arm are all locked into the movement. This action helps to extend the baby's focusing distance from near point to arm's length, from central vision to peripheral vision and back again (see Figures 3.5 and 3.6).

A few days later, the hand may randomly touch an object when extended; over several weeks, as vision is combined with movement, touch and proprioceptive feedback, the infant learns to extend and adjust her focal distance and begins to understand the rudiments of distance, space and time. In other words, what we think of as 'vision' is actually a compound process that has developed over many months of multi-sensory experience entrained through the medium of movement, with the ATNR acting as the first teacher.

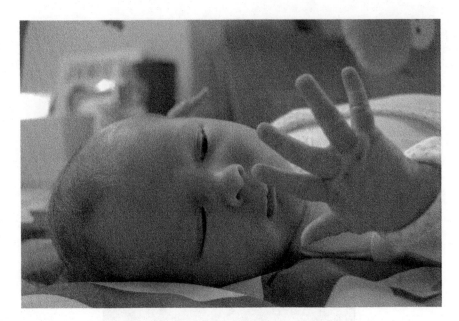

FIGURE 3.5 Eyes focused on centre at near distance

Source: With permission of Hawthorn Press and Wiley Blackwell (Goddard Blythe, 2017).

FIGURE 3.6 Eyes drawn to periphery at far distance

Source: With permission of Hawthorn Press and Wiley Blackwell (Goddard Blythe, 2017).

However, if the ATNR persists beyond infancy, it can interfere in subtle ways with subsequent stages of development, particularly those that involve crossing the midline of the body. These can include:

- difficulty learning to commando crawl;
- difficulty crossing the midline with hand, foot or eyes when the head is turned to the affected side;
- balance.

These apparently minor motor impairments can then affect higher processes involving motor coordination, such as:

- eye tracking (needed to support reading) if Head Righting reflexes are under-developed;
- hand–eye coordination (writing);
- sitting posture when writing;
- development of lateral preference;
- coordination at sports.

The most profound effect of the ATNR on a child in the classroom is usually on handwriting and written work. Because he/she cannot automate the mechanics of writing, additional cognitive effort must be recruited for the task. In effect, this additional effort interferes with the process of translating thoughts on to paper, resulting in a child who is verbally intelligent and articulate but is unable to demonstrate the

FIGURE 3.7 A sitting posture characteristic of a child with ATNR when writing

same amount or quality of knowledge and ideas in written form. This may be the child who is frequently told he/she 'could do better'.

By 6 months of age, the ATNR should be inhibited allowing the infant to move the head freely without influencing muscle tone on either side of the body. This apparently simple development will enable him/her to cross the midline of the body irrespective of head position, to develop independent use of the four quadrants of the body (necessary for crawling) and eventually to have good control of upright balance when the head is turned to either side. In turn, these abilities will facilitate independent and coordinated use of the hand and the eyes needed to write.

If the ATNR is still active in the school-aged child, it can affect visual-motor integration (VMI). Provided the head remains in the middle, there will be no problem, but when the head is turned to follow the writing hand, the arm and hand will extend making it difficult to control the pen or pencil. The child can write, but cannot automate the mechanics of writing.

The Palmar reflex

One of the most recognised of infant reflexes, the Palmar reflex is a reaction to touch or pressure applied to the palm of the hand, which elicits closure of the thumb followed by the fingers into a grip (see Figure 3.1). If you place a finger in the palm of a new born and try to remove it, the grasp becomes tighter. In the first days of life the reflex is strong enough to lift the baby up if he/she is grasping the fingers of both hands.

The Palmar reflex recedes between 3 and 4 months of age to be inhibited by 6 months. Its chief characteristic is involuntary flexion/closure of the hand into a fist grip. If this persists into later childhood it can affect the ability to develop a pincer grip and fine motor control of the hands. Incorrect pen or pencil grip and handwriting deficiency are two of the most common weaknesses associated with a retained Palmar reflex (see Figure 3.8).

In an infant there also exists a reciprocal link between hand and mouth movements, whereby when the infant sucks it elicits small grasping movements in the hands; when the palmar reflex is elicited, it is accompanied by sucking movements in the mouth. This hand–mouth link (Babkin reflex, see Figure 3.9) needs to become uncoupled in the first year of life if the child is to develop independent mouth and hand movements involved in speech and manipulation.

If the link remains active into childhood, it can be associated with:

- speech problems;
- 'overflow' movements, e.g. involuntary mouth movements when writing, using the hand or carrying out other complex tasks;
- over-use of the hands when speaking.

FIGURE 3.8   Immature pencil grip in a child with a Palmar reflex

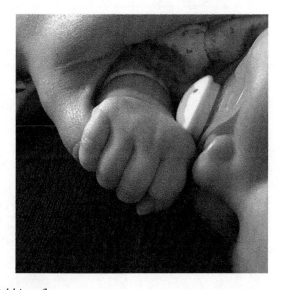

FIGURE 3.9   Babkin reflex

Source: With permission of Hawthorn Press.

Symmetrical Tonic Neck Reflex

The Symmetrical Tonic Neck Reflex (STNR) emerges shortly before an infant is ready to push up on to all fours in preparation for creeping. It is activated in two positions:

1   Head extension when on hands and knees – results in increased extensor tone in the arms and flexion in the legs (see Figure 3.10).
2   Head flexion on hands and knees – results in flexion in the arms and increased extensor tone in the lower half of the body (see Figure 3.11).

Most babies go through a brief phase of 'rocking' on hands and knees, which helps to integrate the reflex so that a few days later they are able to control top and bottom halves of the body irrespective of head position, to support creeping on hands and knees.

Retention of the STNR affects coordination of upper and lower halves of the body depending on the position of the head. When the head is raised, the arms extend and the knees bend; when looking down, the arms bend and the legs want to extend. This can cause problems with sitting posture and sitting still. When

FIGURE 3.10   STNR in extension

Source: With permission of Hawthorn Press.

FIGURE 3.11   STNR in flexion

Source: With permission of Hawthorn Press.

attempting to look down, the arms bend and the child gets closer and closer to the writing surface (see Figure 3.11).

Other signs associated with a retained STNR can include:

- slumped posture when sitting and looking down;
- awkward sitting posture; tendency to wind legs around chair or sit on legs;
- dislike of sitting cross legged;
- poor coordination at gymnastics;
- difficulty learning to swim;
- clumsy, messy eater;
- slow at copying;
- may be present as a feature of Attention Deficit Hyperactivity Disorder (ADHD) (O'Dell & Cook, 2004).

Head Righting Reflexes

As primitive reflexes go through a sequence of activity, inhibition and integration, postural reflexes or reactions develop. Fundamental to the development of good posture, balance and stable visual perception are the Head Righting Reflexes (HRRs).

Head Righting Reflexes are a response to alteration of body position in which the head should automatically 'right' itself to the centre. This righting reaction comprises an equal and opposite correction of head alignment in relation to displacement of the body and its supporting base (see Figures 3.12 and 3.13). This 'top down' adjustment provides a stable reference point or platform for centres involved in the control of eye movements.

Absent or under-developed Head Righting Reflexes in the school-aged child are associated with:

- poor posture;
- immature eye movements;
- visual-perceptual problems leading to under-achievement.

FIGURE 3.12 Developing Head Righting Reflex (HRR)

Source: With permission of Hawthorn Press.

FIGURE 3.13   Absent HRR

Source: With permission of Hawthorn Press.

Relevance of primitive and postural reflexes to education

The examples listed above help to explain how immature primitive and postural reflexes can interfere with various aspects of learning. In short, immature primitive and postural reflexes provide indications of immaturity in the functioning of the central nervous system, and can impede motor dependent aspects of learning.

Most academic learning is connected in some way to motor control and related systems. Reading depends on control of smooth, sequential eye movements, or oculo-*motor* functioning; writing and copying entail hand–eye coordination or visual-*motor* integration; even the ability to sit still and focus attention on one task without being distracted by competing sensory stimuli (freedom from distractibility) involves control of posture and balance. These are the physical foundations for learning. Children with immature postural and motor skills enter the school system under-equipped with the physical *tools* needed for classroom learning, irrespective of intelligence.

Assessment and remediation

Simple tests for balance, coordination and reflexes (that research has consistently shown are features of specific learning difficulties and under-achievement) can help to identify children who may be at risk of under-achieving as a result of immature neuromotor skills.

The concept of introducing physical screening tests into the school system is not new. Until the 1980s every child was assessed by a school medical officer at the time of school entry. Children were asked to stand on one leg, hop across the room, stack bricks and rudimentary tests for vision and hearing were carried out. At the time, there was no system in place to follow up children who did not quite reach all of the expectations, so routine assessment of children's physical skills was phased out. The result has been several generations of children who have been 'lost in the system', neither 'bad enough' to be referred for further assessment, diagnosis and remediation nor 'good enough' to realise their potential in the classroom.

In 1996, I developed a developmental movement programme based upon the INPP clinical programme, designed to be used in schools. Teachers were trained how to carry out a simple screening test for signs of neuro-motor immaturity (NMI) with a class of children at the beginning of the school year, implement the developmental movement programme for 10 minutes every day with the entire class for one academic year, and reassess their neuromotor status at the end of the year. A number of pilot and formal research projects have been carried out on both the screening test and developmental movement programme.

Early pilot projects indicated that there is a relationship between immature neuromotor skills and educational performance. (Pettman, 2000; Bertram, 2002; Micklethwaite, 2004). Larger scale research commissioned by the Department of Education in Northern Ireland, published in a report prepared for the North-Eastern Education Library Board, revealed that in a sample of 663 children in mainstream primary schools in Northern Ireland:

- 35 per cent of P5 children and 48 per cent of P2 children showed elevated levels of retained reflexes at the first assessment.
- 15 per cent (49) of P5 children had a reading age below their chronological age. Of these, 28 also had elevated levels of retained reflexes.
- Elevated levels of retained reflexes are correlated with poor educational achievement at baseline.
- Children who undertook the exercise programme showed a statistically significant greater decrease in retained reflexes than children who did not undertake the exercises.
- Children who undertook the exercise programme showed a highly significant improvement in balance and coordination, and a small but statistically significant increase in a measure of cognitive development over children who did not undertake the exercises.
- No difference was found in reading, handwriting or spelling in children who were already achieving at or near their chronological age, but for children with

high levels of retained reflexes and a reading age below their chronological age, those who undertook the exercise programme made greater progress.

- Retained reflexes are correlated with poor cognitive development, poor balance and teacher assessment of poor concentration/coordination in P2 children.
- Neurological scores and teacher assessment at baseline predicted poorer reading and literacy scores at the end of the study (North Eastern Education and Library Board, 2004, Goddard Blythe, 2005).

Subsequent unpublished projects carried out in primary schools in the Midlands using the INPP screening test and comparing results of the physical tests to national curriculum measures using SATS results, revealed that in a sample of 262 children in Key Stage 1, children who showed some or major issues with measures of neuromotor immaturity were performing below national expectations in reading, writing and numeracy, and vice versa (Goddard Blythe, 2012; Griffin, 2013).

Independent research carried out by physiotherapists in Poland (2017, 2018) using the INPP screening test concluded that 'Introduction of screening tests and treatment of reflex integration at the stage of preschool and early childhood may be a part of the prevention of developmental disorders' (Gieysztor, Sadowska & Choińska, 2017).

After comparing results using the INPP screening test with the Motor Proficiency Test for 4- to 6-year-olds the researchers recommended that:

> It seems reasonable to introduce reflex integration therapy for children with low psychomotor skills. Primitive reflexes, routinely tested, can contribute to improved early psychomotor development in children with needs, thus preventing many difficulties, which children can encounter with their social and school and life.
>
> *(Gieysztor, Choińska & Paprocka-Borowicz, 2016)*

Implications for future policy and research

In Chapter 1, Sir Christopher refers to *new brain sciences*. We now know so much more about the brain, sensory development and the link between movement and learning. It should be stressed that there are many different reasons for specific learning difficulties and educational under-achievement. Not all children presenting with these difficulties will have signs of neuromotor immaturity. Socio-economic factors have a strong influence on educational performance and a teacher's task is to unravel the tangle of factors that might be contributing to a child's frustration and failure in the classroom.

The assessment and potential remediation of signs of neuromotor immaturity are not a replacement for other educational investigations, specialist teaching, learning support or other vital services. They can however, help to identify and remove underlying physical barriers to learning, thereby opening the doors to more effective teaching and learning.

The following excerpt, written by a head teacher who had introduced the INPP screening test into her school in 2013–2014 illustrates how and where the assessment and remediation of neuromotor skills fit into the bigger educational picture and practical application in schools.

> We all know the children in our schools who defy our best efforts to get them to achieve, and yet there is nothing discernible we can put our collective fingers on to 'unlock them' from results that just don't feel right when you spend any time with them having a conversation about their interests and perceptions of life. They may have a cluster of unspecific, but not particularly severe needs, and yet despite your (and their), best efforts, they lag behind on progress and achievement, year on year.

An important part of ensuring that our children start right is understanding the stages of child development and the link between neuro-motor immaturity and potential learning difficulties. The revised early years curriculum proposed by Pat Preedy in Chapter 2 covers from birth to 7 years. It rightly identifies physical development as a specific area of learning, requiring children to have daily opportunities for outside play with movement and multi-sensory learning incorporated into all aspects of learning. The importance of identifying additional needs and early intervention is also included. There should be no excuses for failing to act now.

References

Bender, M., 1976. *Bender-Purdue Reflex test and training manual.* San Rafael, CA: Academic Publications.

Bertram, S., 2002. Learning enhancement through reflex inhibition. Phase 1. Report prepared for The Birmingham Core Skills Partnership.

Beuret, L., 2017. The effects of neuromotor immaturity in adults and adolescents. In: Goddard Blythe, S. A. (Ed.), *Attention, balance and coordination. The A,B,C of learning success* (pp. 280–291). Chichester: Wiley Blackwell.

Blythe, P., & McGlown, D. J., 1979. *An organic basis for educational difficulties and secondary neuroses.* Chester: Insight Publications.

Gieysztor, E. Z., Choi ska, A. M., & Paprocka-Borowicz, M., 2016. Persistence of primitive reflexes and associated motor problems in healthy preschool children. *Archives of Medical Science.* 14/1:167–173. doi: https://doi.org/10.5114/aoms.2016.60503

Gieysztor, E. Z., Sadowska, L., & Choi ska, A. M., 2017. The degree of primitive reflex integration as a diagnostic tool to assess the neurological maturity of healthy preschool and early school age children. *Public Nursing and Public Health.* 26/1:5–11. doi:10.17219/pzp/69471

Goddard Blythe, S. A., 2005. Releasing educational potential through movement. A summary of individual studies carried out using the INPP Test Battery and Developmental Exercise Programme for use in Schools with Children with Special Needs. *Child Care in Practice.* 11/4:415–432.

Goddard Blythe, S. A., 2012. *Assessing neuromotor readiness for learning. The INPP developmental screening test and school intervention programme.* Chichester. Wiley Blackwell.

Goddard Blythe, S. A., 2017. *Attention, balance and coordination. The A B C of learning success* (2nd edn). Chichester: Wiley Blackwell.

Griffin, P., 2013. Neuromotor immaturity (NMI); attainment at Key Stage 1; barrier to learning. www.opendoors-therapy.co.uk

Gustaffsson, D., 1971. A comparison of basic reflexes with the subtests of the Purdue-Perceptual-Motor Survey. Unpublished Master's Thesis, University of Kansas.

McPhillips, M., Hepper, P. G., & Mulhern, G., 2000. Effects of replicating primary reflex movements on specific reading difficulties in children: A randomised, double-blind controlled trial. *Lancet.* 355/2:537–541.

Micklethwaite, J., 2004. A report of a study into the efficacy of the INPP School Programme at Swanwick Primary School, Derbyshire. A controlled study of 93 children. Department for Education and Employment Best Practice Scholarship. www.teachernet.gov.uk

North Eastern Education and Library Board (NEELB), 2004. An evaluation of the pilot INPP movement programme in primary schools in the North-Eastern Education and Library Board. Northern Ireland. Final Report. Prepared by Brainbox Research Ltd. for the NEELB. www.neelb.org.uk

O'Dell, N. E. & Cooke, P. A., 2004. *Stopping ADHD. A unique and proven drug-free program for treating ADHD in children and adults.* New York: Avery.

Pettman, H., 2000. The effects of developmental exercise movements on children with persistent primary reflexes and reading difficulties: A controlled trial (Mellor Primary School, Leicester. Final Report: Best Practice Research Scholarship Study). Department of Education and Skills. www.teachernet.gov.uk

Rider, B., 1976. Relationship of postural reflexes to learning disabilities. *American Journal of Occupational Therapy.* 26/5:239–243.

Taylor, M., Houghton, S., & Chapman, E., 2004. Primitive reflexes and attention-deficit/hyperactivity disorder: developmental origins of classroom dysfunction. *International Journal of Special Education.* 19/1:23–37.

4

MOVEMENT FOR LEARNING

Rebecca Duncombe and Pat Preedy

Introduction

Chapter 3 highlighted the links between physical and cognitive development and the potential impact of neuro-immaturity and potential learning difficulties. As discussed in Chapter 2, physical development is a core component of the current (2017) Early Years Foundation Stage Framework (EYFS) and is described within this document as being one of three prime areas 'particularly crucial for igniting children's curiosity and enthusiasm for learning, and for building their capacity to learn, form relationships and thrive' (Department for Education, 2017, p. 7). The other two prime areas (communication and language; and personal, social and emotional development) appear to be allocated equal importance within the discourse generated from this document. However, the authors were becoming increasingly aware that something was *amiss* in relation to young children's physical development and the opportunities provided for them in this area. While the EYFS identifies the components of Physical Development within the early years as: 'providing opportunities for young children to be active and interactive, and to develop their co-ordination, control, and movement. Children must also be helped to understand the importance of physical activity, and to make healthy choices in relation to food' (Department for Education, 2017, p. 8), reports from teachers and the authors' own observations were portraying a different picture. Moreover, media coverage in recent years frequently claims that: academic standards are falling (e.g. *The Telegraph*, 2013); children aren't school ready (e.g. *The Telegraph*, 2014; *Mail Online*, 2016; *Mail Online*, 2017; BBC, 2017); and the incidence of a number of neurodevelopmental disorders appears to be on the increase (e.g. *The Telegraph*, 2010; *Mail Online* 2010). Likewise, there are regular reports that obesity and sedentary behaviour are on the increase and that many children are not physically active enough to benefit their health. For example, the most recent data from the National Child Measurement

Programme informs us that in 2016/2017, 9.6 per cent of reception children were obese (NHS Digital, 2017). Similarly, in a document published by the British Heart Foundation in 2015 (Townsend, Wickramasinghe, Williams, Bhatnagar & Rayner, 2015), it is reported that just 9 per cent of boys and 10 per cent of girls (aged 2–4) were meeting the UK Physical activity guidelines of 180 minutes of physical activity a day (discussed further in the following section).

With this as the driving force, the authors embarked upon the *Movement for Learning* project (2015–2017) in order to explore four key research questions:

1   Has physical development (upon entry to school in reception – age 4–5 years) declined in recent years?
2   Can a daily movement programme help to improve physical development and reduce retained primitive reflexes in reception children?
3   Are there any relationships between levels of physical development and retained primitive reflexes in young children?
4   What is the impact of a daily movement programme upon learning/behaviour in the foundation stage?

The *Movement for Learning* project was developed by Pat Preedy (Former head teacher, Early Years researcher and consultant), Rebecca Duncombe (former primary school teacher and PE specialist) and Joanne Duston (an Occupational Therapist working in an independent school). The programme was piloted in two schools in 2015–2016, revised, and then delivered in 20 schools (2016–2017). Baseline and end of intervention data were collected for 120 children from four schools across the two years and anecdotal feedback provided by 15 teachers via an online survey (summer 2017).

Background to the project

The requirements of the physical development component of the EYFS are outlined above but what does this mean in practice? What 'movement' opportunities are our young children engaged in during their early years? Helpful, but arguably limited, guidance comes from the Department of Health Physical Activity guidelines (2011), which state that young children capable of walking in the 0–5 age range should be moderately to vigorously active for 180 minutes a day and spend minimal time engaged in sedentary activities. Suggested activities within this document include:

•   activities that involve movements of all the major muscle groups, i.e. the legs, buttocks, shoulders and arms, and movement of the trunk from one place to another;
•   energetic play, e.g. climbing frame or riding a bike;
•   more energetic bouts of activity, e.g. running and chasing games;
•   walking/skipping to shops, a friend's home, a park or to and from a school.

sical activity is not the same as physical development (although one
...d to the other) and while this guidance provides a helpful starting point in
terms of the quantity of physical activity young children should be doing to benefit
their health, it does not go far enough to highlight *what* young children should be
doing to improve their physical development. Taking the information from this (the
Department of Health physical activity recommendations) and the EYFS guidance,
it is possible to see why practitioners may find it difficult to provide appropriate
activities in their settings and, in turn, why young children's physical development
may be underdeveloped; a problem perhaps exacerbated by the limited amount of
training that practitioners receive in this area.

The Physical Development component of the EYFS is divided into two sections: Moving and Handling, and Health and Self Care and, within the Moving and
Handling aspect of this, children should: 'Show good control and co-ordination in
large and small movements . . . move confidently in a range of ways, safely negotiat-
ing space . . . handle equipment and tools effectively, including pencils for writing'
(Department for Education, 2017, p. 11).

Further guidance can be found (if you are so inclined and have the time) within
another document produced by the British Association for Early Childhood Education: 'Development Matters in the Early Years Foundation Stage'. This is described
as 'non-statutory guidance material' to support 'practitioners in implementing the
statutory requirements of the EYFS' (British Association for Early Childhood Education, 2012, p. 1). Within this, each of three prime areas is taken in turn and example activities are offered along with what adults can do to facilitate each activity and
how the environment of the setting could be adapted to encourage it. For example,
a child aged 8–20 months might be expected to be able to do the following:

- sit unsupported on the floor;
- when sitting, can lean forward to pick up small toys;
- pulls to standing, holding on to furniture or person for support;
- crawls, bottom shuffles[1] or rolls continuously to move around;
- walks around furniture lifting one foot and stepping sideways (cruising), and
  walks with one or both hands held by adult;
- takes first few steps independently;
- passes toys from one hand to the other;
- holds an object in each hand and brings them together in the middle, e.g. holds
  two blocks and bangs them together;
- picks up small objects between thumb and fingers;
- enjoys the sensory experience of making marks in damp sand, paste or paint;
- holds pen or crayon using a whole hand (palmar) grasp and makes random
  marks with different strokes.

(British Association for Early Childhood Education, 2012, p. 22)

An arguably clearer picture of what is expected of young children at different
ages emerges from this document. However, it is still not easy to 'extract' exactly

what young children should be doing on a daily basis and how these opportunities might be offered within the logistical confines of a nursery or pre-school (or indeed within the home).

It is possible using the current EYFS documentation to glean a vague idea of what young children should be doing in terms of their physical development. However, this information is piecemeal and not always clearly transferable into practice. Linking this back to the concerns regarding physical readiness to start school identified by the authors in previous chapters, the lack of clear guidance for practitioners may be one contributory factor. Additional factors, which will not be explored in depth here, include (amongst other things): concerns over young children's increasing exposure to screen time; increased use of equipment that forces the child into developmentally inappropriate positions; a lack of tummy-time; decreasing amounts of outdoor play; over-reliance on cars for travelling; and the general lack of status afforded to Physical Education, Physical Activity and Physical Development within society more broadly. With this background, the *Movement for Learning* project was developed to establish whether physical development had declined in recent years and, if yes, to ascertain whether a daily movement programme could contribute to reversing this.

The *Movement for Learning* programme

The *Movement for Learning* programme was designed to provide a range of movement experiences that children may have missed during their early development. It contributes to the physical development component of the Early Years curriculum and is not intended to replace other physical activities or Physical Education (PE).

Specific exercises are delivered to the whole class on a daily basis using equipment normally found in schools such as beanbags and hoops. The programme is divided into six units of activities and each session comprises:

- warm up with specific movements;
- activities using equipment;
- cool down combined with letter formation, articulating sounds and listening to classical music to improve auditory processing.

The daily session lasts approximately 15–20 minutes including time to get ready and to move to and from the hall. Children participate in their normal school clothes but with bare feet (removing ties and jumpers). The key to the programme is that it is run daily with repetition of the movements over the 4-week period. This pattern gives children the opportunity to practise and improve the quality of each movement. Figures 4.1 and 4.3 illustrate the programme in action in the two pilot schools.

The Movement for Learning *pilot*

The purpose of the pilot phase was to assess whether the programme *worked* in a school context and to establish whether it had an impact on children's

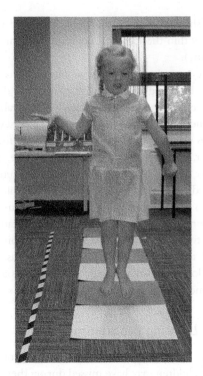

FIGURE 4.1 Movement for Learning assessment

FIGURE 4.2 *Movement for Learning* in a state school

development. Two schools participated during the pilot phase of the research (2015–2016):

- School A: a state primary school located in the Midlands (England):
    - Two classes were involved in the research (the intervention and the comparison group).
- School B: an independent school located within the Yorkshire region (England):
    - Due to the low number of children and there only being one class, a comparison group was not possible in this school.

The research was run in collaboration with Loughborough University and the necessary ethical procedures adhered to. Participating pupils were assessed towards the end of their first month in reception (2015) and then again towards the end of the academic year (2016) to allow baseline and end of intervention comparisons to be made. Assessments included The Movement Assessment Battery for Children (Barnett, Henderson & Sugden, 2007), which enables scores for balance, manual dexterity and aiming/catching to be calculated, and an overall physical development score to be produced. The Institute of Neuro Physiological Psychology screening tests (Goddard Blythe, 2012) were also used in order to identify retained primitive reflexes and potential visual-motor integration problems. Towards the end of the academic year, teachers from both schools were interviewed within a small focus group at School B to further explore the nature of the impact of the programme and whether any changes to the programme might be needed in the revised version.

The Movement for Learning *research data*

The data presented here will be used to answer two of the research questions identified earlier in the chapter:

- Has physical development (upon entry to school in reception) declined in recent years?
- Can a daily movement programme help to improve physical development and reduce retained primitive reflexes in reception children?

In order to answer the first question, the authors compared the baseline data from this cohort of children with 'norms' established by the authors of the Movement ABC when they calculated their percentile scores in 2007. Percentile scores are commonly used for height and weight and the norm would be around the 50th percentile with those falling above the 75th percentile, for example, being seen as tall for their age and those falling below the 25th percentile as short. Thus, it would be expected for a cohort of children to have a mean around the 50th percentile and for some children to score better and some worse. A child with a significant movement difficulty is identified within the Movement ABC as falling at or below the

5th percentile and a child at risk of a movement difficulty would fall between the 6th and 15th percentile. Clearly, we would want our children to be above the 50th percentile and towards the 100th but children scoring above the 16th percentile are not identified as a cause for concern within this assessment.

Data were collected for 46 children in the pilot phase and the findings presented below:

- *Balance*: 9.5 per cent of the participating children scored below the 16th percentile.
- *Manual dexterity*: 36.4 per cent of the participating children scored below the 16th percentile.
- *Aiming and catching*: 51.5 per cent of the participating children scored below the 16th percentile.
- *Overall physical development score*: 28.9 per cent of the participating children scored below the 16th percentile.

To be in line with the 2007 data, we would expect the percentages outlined above to be around 16 per cent, thus, balance within our cohort does seem somewhat better than in 2007 but all other scores are noticeably worse and almost double the number of children in our sample (28.9 per cent) scored below the 16th percentile for overall physical development, indicating a decline since 2007. While the numbers involved in this pilot are low (46), an initial analysis of the phase 2 data (120 children) reveals a very similar picture across four different schools.

It was also possible to use the INPP screening tests to explore whether physical development has declined in recent years. Whilst there are no available data from previous years to use as a comparison (as with the Movement ABC), it is possible to state whether the children in our sample were able to achieve age-appropriate expectations. A core element of the INPP screening tests is the primitive reflex tests, which indicate immaturity in the central nervous system (this is expanded upon in greater detail in Chapter 3): 'Neurodevelopmental delay describes the continued presence of a cluster of primitive reflexes in a child above 6 months of age together with absent or under-developed postural reflexes above the age of 3.5' (Goddard Blythe, 2009, p. 4). As all of the children in our pilot study were above 3.5 years of age, we would not expect to observe a positive result on any of these tests. Worryingly, we found the following:

- Tonic Labyrinthine Reflex (TLR): this was found to be retained at 50 per cent or more in 75 per cent of the children tested and was fully retained in 39.3 per cent.
- Asymmetrical Tonic Neck Reflex (ATNR): this was found to be retained at 50 per cent or more in 89 per cent of the children tested and was fully retained in 29.6 per cent.
- Symmetrical Tonic Neck Reflex (STNR): this was found to be retained at 50 per cent or more in 83 per cent of the children tested and was fully retained in 28.8 per cent.

Combining together the findings from the two assessments, a fairly negative picture of the state of young children's physical development is revealed. It could be argued that despite their participation in the EYFS during the 'nursery years', many of these children have arrived at school lacking the physical skills necessary to be successful in the classroom.

Bearing this in mind, we turn to the second research question: Can a daily movement programme help to improve physical development and reduce retained primitive reflexes in reception children?

As previously, the Movement ABC data will be examined first. We know from the baseline data reported above that almost 30 per cent of the participating pupils were identified as having or being at risk of a movement difficulty (those scoring below the 16th percentile for overall physical development). Having completed the *Movement for Learning* programme the following changes were observed:

The findings presented above indicate that participation in the *Movement for Learning* programme may help to decrease the number of children with or at risk of a movement difficulty (i.e. those who fall below the 16th percentile). Likewise, not participating in the programme and just being exposed to the normal EYFS curriculum would not seem to be enough to improve the physical development of these young children.

Looking now to the reflex scores and a reminder that our baseline data revealed a large proportion of children starting school with their primitive reflexes retained at 50 per cent or more. The *Movement for Learning* programme was never designed to be a reflex inhibition programme. It was designed to allow children an opportunity

TABLE 4.1 Impact of *Movement for Learning*: comparison of the Movement ABC data

Percentage of children scoring below the 16th percentile at baseline	Percentage of children scoring below the 16th percentile at the end of the year	Difference
School A intervention class		
30.4%	18.2%	12.2% improved enough to no longer have or be at risk of a movement difficulty
School A comparison class		
27.3%	31.8%	**4.5% got worse** over the year and became at risk of or had a movement difficulty
School B (no comparison data)		
42.9%	28.6%	14.3% improved enough to no longer have or be at risk of a movement difficulty

FIGURE 4.3 Movement for Learning in an Independent School

to spend time on the floor on their backs and tummies engaging in developmentally appropriate exercises and activities and, due to this, there was of course a chance that these might impact the reflexes to some degree. The data presented below show that reflex scores improved for the intervention groups but got worse for those not doing the programme.

Both assessments (The Movement ABC and the INPP screening tests) confirm that participation in a daily movement programme can help to improve physical development and reduce retained primitive reflexes in Reception children and that, conversely, participation solely in the EYFS curriculum may lead to declines in physical development. These are clearly *grand* claims based on low numbers, but this was the situation, as we found it, in the two schools that we worked with during the pilot phase and within two additional schools that we worked in during the following year (as demonstrated by a preliminary analysis). After a year of participation in a daily movement programme, pupils are not physical development *superstars* but the additional input does seem to put them back on track and bring them back in line with norms established in 2007 (certainly as far as the Movement ABC data is concerned).

The data presented above were supported by comments from the teachers involved during a focus group interview conducted with teachers at both schools and these comments also help to illustrate some of the broader ways in which

TABLE 4.2 Comparison of children with retained reflex scores of 50 per cent or more at the start and end of the project

Percentage of children with reflex retained at 50% or more

	TLR		ATNR		STNR	
	Baseline	*End*	*Baseline*	*End*	*Baseline*	*End*
School A intervention	75%	62.5%	91.7%	66.7%	86.4%	86.4%
School A comparison	72.7%	**95.5%**	81.8%	**100%**	71.4%	**100%**
School B intervention	77.8%	55.6%	100%	87.5%	100%	87.5%

TABLE 4.3 Comparison of children with retained reflex scores of 100 per cent at the start and end of the project

Percentage of children with reflex retained at 100%

	TLR		ATNR		STNR	
	Baseline	*End*	*Baseline*	*End*	*Baseline*	*End*
School A intervention	37.5%	8.3%	33.3%	8.3%	27.3%	18.2%
School A comparison	36.4%	**59.1%**	27.3%	**31.8%**	23.8%	**57.1%**
School B intervention	55.6%	11.1%	25%	12.5%	37.5%	0%

Movement for Learning had an impact within the classroom. The following improvements were observed across the two schools:

- balance;
- muscle tone, stamina, suppleness and gross motor movements;
- posture and control;
- body and sensory awareness;
- grip and fine motor movements;
- self-control, persistence and organisation;
- language, rhythm and communication skills;
- attention, listening and processing of sound;
- independence, leadership and team work;
- self-esteem and confidence.

The interviews were recorded, transcribed and analysed, and the following comments were of particular interest:

> [I]n the sessions, their concentration is just, it's so focused on what we're doing from 98% of the children, 98% of the time, the concentration from them is incredible and I think you're seeing more of that in the classroom. So, when they're doing their independent learning, they're not as needy of adult support because they can concentrate on it a bit longer than they would perhaps be able to do otherwise.
>
> I think that when it comes to, for example sports day, and we always do a skipping race and the parents always love watching them trying to do their skipping, and we've never done it as individual skipping with the rope. Well actually, this year, I think those children could manage it.
>
> I have seen a great difference in some children's balance and co-ordination from taking part in daily MfL. It amazes me how quickly you can fit it into your daily routine.
>
> We've got three out of twenty seven this year who are finding letter formation tricky, whereas normally, at this point, there are still ten who are spider writing and you can't read what they have written. So I think it has made an impact on their writing, particularly their letter formation.

The project was named *Movement for Learning* to give the message that movement is an essential component of children's development and learning. Feedback from teachers indicates that the improvements seen through the two assessments were also observed in the classroom in a variety of ways across the curriculum.

Future developments of the project

The data presented here were produced during the pilot phase of the project (2015–2016). The following year (2016–2017) a further two schools were included as full research schools and approximately 20 schools delivered *Movement for Learning* to their Reception children. An online survey was sent out to teachers towards the end of the academic year (June, 2017) and these data will help the authors to further explore the nature of the impact of the project. Likewise, the data from the two additional research schools will enable a collated analysis of approximately 120 children. Where possible, academic data will also be collected from the schools and analysed to establish whether those who participated in the programme progressed further from their 'academic' baseline than those who didn't.

The research element of the project is nearing its conclusion. The data indicating the benefits of the programme are now available to all schools at no cost. Further details regarding registration can be found at www.movementforlearning-project.co.uk. A Year One programme for children aged 5–6 years is also available at no cost on this website. Our aim is to contribute to the re-definition of early childhood education by enabling as many schools and children as possible to benefit from the research by integrating movement into all aspects of learning.

Discussion

The findings from this research support the authors' beliefs, teachers' observations and media reports that physical development has declined in recent years. It was possible to compare our data with norms established in 2007 and, within the two schools where the research was conducted, there was almost double the proportion of children starting school with or at risk of significant movement difficulties (than would have been the case in 2007). Earlier in this chapter a number of reasons were identified for why this might be. It is worrying that physical development seems to have declined since the introduction of the EYFS in 2008 despite physical development being a prime area within this framework.

It would also seem that a daily movement programme can become part of daily life in a school and also be effective in improving physical development. Sadly, however, programmes such as *Movement for Learning* are a response to things that have already gone wrong and it would be better for us to focus our efforts on getting things right from the start, as proposed by Preedy in her revised Early Years Curriculum Framework (Chapter 2).

At the heart of this change is the need for a better understanding of what we mean by physical development, how best to provide opportunities for our young children to engage with developmentally appropriate activities and for practitioners and parents to be more aware of what a physically developed child looks like and when a child has delayed physical development that requires early intervention. Physical development needs to be recognised as underpinning academic success and the reasons for this need to be communicated widely. In the meantime, we would put forward *Movement for Learning* (and other similar movement programmes) as one way in which we can help children reach their physical and, in turn, their academic potential.

References

Barnett, A., Henderson, S. E. & Sugden, D. A. (2007). *Movement Assessment Battery for Children – Second Edition (Movement ABC-2)*. Pearson: London.

BBC (2017). *Too many new pupils not school ready, say head teachers* www.bbc.co.uk/news/education-41160919

British Association for Early Childhood Education (2012). *Development Matters in the Early Years Foundation Stage (EYFS)*. Early Education: London.

British Heart Foundation (2015). Physical Activity Statistics 2015.

Department for Education (2017). *Statutory framework for the early years foundation stage: Setting the standards for learning, development and care for children from birth to five.* London: DfE

Department of Health (2011). *Start active, stay active: A report on physical activity for health from the four home countries' Chief Medical Officers.* Available: https://www.gov.uk/government/uploads/system/uploads/attachment_data/file/216370/dh_128210.pdf

Goddard Blythe, S. (2009). *Attention, Balance and Coordination – the A,B,C of Learning Success.* Oxford: Wiley–Blackwell.

Goddard Blythe, S. (2012). *Assessing Neuromotor Readiness for Learning: The INPP Developmental Screening Test and School Intervention Programme.* Oxford: Wiley Blackwell.

Macintyre, C. (2000). *Dyspraxia in the Early Years.* London: Fulton.

Mail Online (2010). A Special Needs label on fifth of all children: double that of 20 years ago www.dailymail.co.uk/news/article-1296678/A-special-needs-label-fifth-children.html

Mail Online (2016). Thousands of children lacking in school readiness www.dailymail.co.uk/wires/pa/article-3580133/Thousands-children-lacking-school-readiness.html

Mail Online (2017). Many new pupils not school ready, Head teachers say. www.dailymail.co.uk/wires/pa/article-4856884/Many-new-pupils-not-school-ready-headteachers-say.html

NHS Digital (2017). National Child Measurement Programme: England, 2016–17. NHS Digital.

The Telegraph (2010). More children have special needs www.telegraph.co.uk/education/educationnews/7720653/More-children-have-special-educational-needs.html

The Telegraph (2013). SATS results 2013: quarter of pupils struggling in three Rs. www.telegraph.co.uk/education/educationnews/10319870/Sats-results-2013-quarter-of-pupils-struggling-in-three-Rs.html

The Telegraph (2014). Half of children are not ready to start school www.telegraph.co.uk/news/uknews/11113837/Half-of-children-are-not-ready-to-start-school.html

Townsend, N., Wickramasinghe, K., Williams, J., Bhatnagar, P., & Rayner, M. (2015). *Physical Activity Statistics 2015.* British Heart Foundation: London.

5

DO PARENTS NEED TO BE QUALIFIED?

Pat Preedy and Rosie Hamilton McGinty

The Start Right Report (Ball, 1994) emphasised the importance of parents to children's learning and development, highlighting what was termed a *triangle of care* between parents, professionals and the community. The recommendations to have a public debate on the subject of parenthood in order to establish exemplifications of good practice based on research and proven experience, and the provision of systematic and appropriate education to enable parents to fulfil their role effectively were not taken forward. In Chapter 1 of this book, Sir Christopher Ball presents a strong case that the education and support of parents is an area that still needs to be addressed. He acknowledges that at the time of the report some of the contributors dissociated themselves from paragraphs 5.8 and 5.9 as they did not agree with statements promoting the importance of fathers and high risks associated with single parenthood and broken parenthood. However, since 1994 there have been huge positive changes in attitudes towards gender and race underpinned by Equality legislation. Time has not weakened Sir Christopher's message, but it has rounded it with references to choosing a reliable and long-term partner, and to providing what children need using the mnemonic NESTLE (Nurture, Exercise, Stimulation, Talk, Love and an Environment that is stimulating and safe). The further suggestions he makes for parents are sensible and difficult to take issue with:

- Before starting a pregnancy ensure that you are both in good health, and have a good enough home for the baby to share with you.
- Lead by example – demonstrate the virtues of self-reliance, strong families and the learning habit.
- Foster curiosity and independence, while always providing a framework of security and protection for the young child.
- Learn to practise 'tough' love.
- Study and prepare for the demanding work of parenting.

- Create a supportive partnership with your child's school(s), the teachers and your friends (and theirs), to develop the 'triangle of care' that is essential for good long-term nurture of the young.

The final three recommendations Sir Christopher leaves to the reader and our grandchildren. This chapter seeks to support the reader in reflecting upon what these recommendations might be.

Working in partnership with parents is a requirement of the EYFS and an aspect that is judged as part of inspection. Most schools and settings welcome parents, sharing information about organisation, the curriculum and assessments. There are several courses available for parents such as through the national parenting initiative. However, in order to implement fully the *triangle of care*, we believe schools and settings have a key role in providing *a course* for parents that focuses on the essential elements of effective parenting. Rather than develop a course from a curriculum perspective we set out to develop a course that goes to the heart of learning – personal, social and emotional development.

A Winning Attitude (Hamilton-McGinty, 2000) had already been published using a variety of positive quotes intended to change lives by changing attitudes. Using the same principle of changing lives by changing attitudes, we devised *A Winning Attitude* course for the parents of young children up to 7 years of age. A school or setting is able to provide the course in one day or as a series of workshops. We were pleased that the course was endorsed by Cache, which meant that teachers and practitioners running the course would receive a Cache endorsed certificate. Parents would also receive a certificate of attendance. The two pilot sessions held at Pattison College, Coventry and The Revel Primary School, Rugby were very well received. The following were typical comments from parents;

> *A very informative day led by extremely knowledgeable practitioners. We would highly recommend the course to other parents.*
> *I will be going home and making positive changes including being a play partner with my daughter.*
> *It was good to talk to other parents about how they manage such things as children having tantrums and refusing to eat.*

Feedback from staff indicated that some of them lacked confidence and did not feel that they always had the knowledge and experience to answer parental questions. We therefore published an e-book addressing questions typically raised by parents covering topics such as aggression, anxiety, toilet training and enuresis, bullying, divorce and separation, encouraging good behaviour, sleeping difficulties, eating problems, stealing, bereavement, temper tantrums, twins and higher multiples (Hamilton-McGinty and Preedy, 2017). We also designed a short on-line course for teachers and practitioners through *Laser Learning*, which provides those delivering the course with the necessary underpinning knowledge and skills explored further in this chapter.

What is parenting?

Parenting is the process of supporting the physical, emotional, spiritual, social and intellectual development of a child from infancy to adulthood through a bond of love that is often described as attachment.

John Bowlby (1988, 2010) has brought much to our understanding of attachment. His work as a psychiatrist in a child guidance clinic in London, where he treated many emotionally disturbed children, led him to consider the importance of the child's relationship with their mother in terms of their social, emotional and cognitive development. Working with Mary Ainsworth, he concluded that attachment is a deep and enduring emotional bond that connects one person to another across time and space.

Initially the baby needs a specific attachment for security, comfort and protection. He or she shows fear of strangers and unhappiness when separated from a special person (separation anxiety). Some babies show stranger fear and separation anxiety much more frequently and intensely than others. From 10 months the baby becomes increasingly independent and forms several attachments so that by 18 months most infants have formed multiple attachments.

Attachments are most likely to form with those who respond warmly and accurately to the baby's signals. In Chapter 1 Sir Christopher describes how to 'NESTLE' a child by providing Nurture, Exercise, Stimulation, Talk, Love and an Environment indoors and outdoors that is stimulating and safe. Securely attached children use their attachment figure as a secure base from which they can explore, but return to in times of distress where they are easily comforted and soon return to play. Attachment behaviour in adults towards the child includes responding sensitively and appropriately to the child's needs. We can observe how the adult uses touch, voice and looks to show that the child is loved, safe and cared for.

The way we parent is mostly learned from our parents or carers. Parents do not have to be perfect, but it is important that they strive to be *good* parents taking responsibility for ensuring that children have access to the key elements that they need – a process often referred to as nurturing. Field (2010) highlights that children need nurturing for longer than the young of any other species and that it is the aspirations and actions of parents that are critical to how well their children prosper.

Why is parenting so important?

Parenting is vitally important because the combination of support and structure that it provides enables children to develop the personal, social and emotional skills that they need for successful learning and life. The Start Right Report (Ball, 1994) recognised the importance of parents placing them at the top of the pecking order: 'Parents are the most important people in their children's lives. It is from parents that children learn most, particularly in the early months and years' (Ball, 1994, p. 43).

Children who receive sensitive and consistent responses from parents who are *warm demanders* (Ball, 1994) are able to thrive on a foundation of trust and security.

From this secure base they are able to develop self-regulation, relationships and appropriate emotional responses. In his recommendations for parenting Sir Christopher suggests *tough love* as being important. Steinberg et al. (1992) found that children who experienced authoritative parenting where parents consistently have high expectations with a firm but fair style achieve more in school, report less depression and anxiety, and tend to score higher on measures of self-reliance and self-esteem. They are also less likely to engage in antisocial behaviours such as delinquency and drug use.

Hughes and Baylin (2012) describe how various parts of the brain are activated during parenting with systems that enable the fundamental aspects of care needed by children. *The Parental Approach System* is defined as the system that enables parents to be close to their children in an open and engaged relationship. If children's behaviour is challenging then parents may perceive this as threatening, triggering a defensive withdrawal response associated with the amygdala. *The Parental Reward System* describes the pleasure that it is possible for parents to experience from parenting. This is linked to *The Parental Child Reading System*, which enables the parent to understand and attune with the child's inner subjective experiences and what he or she is conveying non-verbally. A positive experience of parenting enables parents to construct a working narrative about being a parent and to develop *The Parental Executive System*, which is associated with the prefrontal cortex. These higher-level functions enable parents to monitor their feelings and actions enabling them to respond more effectively and in an attuned way to the child. Conversely, parents under stress may block their capacity to sustain loving feelings and empathy towards the child. This situation can be related to the parent's own childhood experiences where he or she has not experienced positive and loving parenting, which is also a preparation for when the child becomes a parent. *Blocking* can also be related to a traumatic experience such as death or to a particular stage that the child is going through e.g. the terrible twos. From the child's perspective, *blocking* may lead to feelings of shame, anger and controlling behaviours. In order to protect himself or herself against these feelings of shame the child may exhibit behaviours such as rage, lying, blaming others or trying to minimise events in order to appear less responsible for what is happening.

Parenting is important for the emotional development of the child and the parent. It is key to the child feeling safe, developing self-esteem and resilience and being able to build relationships that are underpinned by the giving and receiving of care. Above all it is the blueprint for when the child becomes a parent himself or herself, sub-consciously drawing upon and often replicating his or her earlier experiences.

Has parenting changed?

Although society has changed and is changing, for many children parenting has not changed as we tend to replicate the type of parenting that we have experienced. In recent times social media has revolutionised the way people work and

FIGURE 5.1   *Good* parenting enables the child to feel safe and to build relationships

communicate, and the roles of women and men have been blurred with a variety of family models including single and same-sex parents. Parents today are faced with many challenges including supporting children financially and affording child-care. Many parents feel that it is impossible to provide for their children without both of them working, while others struggle to allow one parent to stay at home. More and more parents are asking for advice about how to be a *good* parent.

What is good parenting?

The Demos report 'Building Character' (Lexmond and Reeves, 2009) identifies strong links between parenting style and the character development of children. The report analysed data from over 9,000 households highlighting that children aged 0–3 years were more influenced by parents than at any other age. It found that in the UK 8 per cent of families (600,000 families) had parents who were *disengaged*. These families were also most likely to be found amongst low-income groups. The case for supporting parents is even stronger than it was in 1994.

Good parenting is about providing a warm, secure home life, helping children to learn the rules of life, how to share, respect others and to develop self-esteem. Good parenting is the raising of children willingly accepting the responsibilities and activities that are involved with their development until they reach adulthood. Golding (2017) suggests that good parenting is about PACE:

- *Playfulness*: everything can be play; plan time to play together (we see from Chapters 4 and 6 that 10 minutes a day can have an enormous impact;

FIGURE 5.2 Finding time to play with your child is part of *good* parenting

- *Acceptance*: give lots of praise; be proud of your child; help him or her to grow in confidence and self-esteem;
- *Curiosity*; wonder, ask questions and find out together;
- *Empathy*; feel with your child, helping him or her to understand and regulate feelings and behaviour.

A wide body of international research consistently highlights the positive impact of parents regularly and naturally interacting and engaging with their children. Professor Charles Deforges (Deforges and Abouchaar, 2003) concluded that the more parents and children talk to each other about meaningful subjects, the better children achieve both in the short term and the long term. The importance of parents engaging with their children has also been emphasised in an in-depth meta-analysis of the influences on pupil learning. Hattie (2008) conducted a 15-year analysis of 50,000 studies involving 83 million students to see what worked in education. The findings indicated that consistent engagement between parent and child can:

- add the equivalent of 2–3 years of formal education;
- result in higher grades and test scores;
- improve confidence, attitude, attendance, life choices, social skills, behaviour and effort.

Engaging with children is a key element of attachment. Play is the natural way to engage with young children. By sharing, encouraging and talking with their children, parents are able to deepen their attachment and long-term relationship thus providing the foundations for the child's personal, social and emotional development and his or her long-term outcomes. Chapter 6 describes how parents can engage with their children using the *play partners* method.

The style of behaviour that is natural to a child is often described as his or her temperament. Young children have different levels of reactivity with regard to the following aspects:

- amount of physical movement;
- length of time they can pay attention;
- level of distress displayed;
- amount of positive reactions they give, e.g. smiling.

Adults frequently respond more to children who smile and appear to have more positive body language and less to children who are not as responsive. This reduces the amount of parental engagement for some children, and can adversely affect the attachment of both the adult and the child leading to less engagement with weaker attachment.

Rules are an important part of everyday life and good parenting. They make it possible to get along with one another. Children who do not learn how to self-regulate and to keep simple agreed rules will find it difficult to get on both with grown-ups and with other children – particularly when they start nursery or school.

Children who are struggling to manage their behaviour often display one or more of the following behaviours:

- withdrawal;
- aggression;
- hyperactivity.

It is important not to label a child as *naughty*. Often when children appear to misbehave it is because we are not providing appropriately for their stage of development. Rather than labelling the child, think about how to meet his or her emotional and developmental needs by:

- providing activities that are not too difficult and can be done in different ways; this enables the child to experience success rather than frustration;
- changing situation particularly enabling outside play;
- choosing a time when the child is less excitable to introduce an activity that requires concentration;
- keeping stories and songs short and interesting; seating the child near to them and using their voice and body language to make the experience fun;
- avoiding over stimulation; limiting the number of toys and materials; tidying away together before moving on to the next activity;
- giving structure: helping children to plan and organise their activities.

Mutual respect and courtesy are important for building strong relationships. Children copy behaviour and it is essential that adults provide good role models and continually praise *good* behaviour with specific language e.g. *I like how you are picking up your toys and putting them in the box.*

Consistency enables children to make sense of their world and to feel secure. As a family, agree the rules that everyone (including the adults) are expected to abide by. For example:

- We always say *Please* and *Thank you.*
- Our evening routine is bath, story and bed by 7 pm.
- We do not leave the table until the meal is finished.
- We tidy away our toys.

Parents frequently ask for advice about managing challenging behaviour and tantrums. Successfully managing behaviour starts from having a secure attachment based upon a warm and loving relationship, combined with structure and boundaries. Although control can be enforced without love and empathy – it is short-term and builds resentment. As Golding (2017) highlights, *there can be no correction without connection.*

Adults must never use physical punishments, shouting, verbal humiliation or locking in rooms as a way to manage children's behaviour. As well as destroying secure attachments, the child is likely to replicate this behaviour and so perpetuate a negative cycle. Adults need opportunities to learn about what is normal behaviour for young children and ways of re-directing behaviour with appropriate consequences. The following are some helpful strategies:

- Ask the child why he or she has behaved in this way. The answer may show that the child was not deliberately misbehaving. For example, when a Mum asked her son why he had tipped the cereals out of the cupboard, he replied that he was making breakfast for her. The Mum sat down and enjoyed breakfast with her son and then they cleared up together.
- Removing a sticker from a chart is not fair when good behaviour has earnt this. Try using a chart where an object is moved for positive behaviour. The child then wants to change his or her behaviour to move further up the chart towards a reward.
- Removing the child from the situation (time-out) is often effective. However, time out means moving the child to a place to think about being good (never the naughty step or chair). Keep the child in view and be ready to support him or her in apologising and moving on.
- Reducing a treat is often more effective than removing the treat all together.

For many adults, low income and poor housing make it even more challenging to be a good parent. For those working, time is frequently constrained, and stress increased due to heavy workloads and family commitments. More sedentary

FIGURE 5.3   Everyday activities provide opportunities for play and learning

lifestyles, the demand for commercial toys and the explosion of technology into all aspects of life are adversely impacting many children's opportunities to play physically and creatively. *A Winning Attitude* workshop uses the *Play Partners* research developed by Professor Pat Preedy and Dr Kay Sanderson (described in detail in Chapter 6), which provides parents with an easy, fun and effective way of engaging with their children. The *Play Partners* method uses everyday activities such as cooking, bath-time, doing the laundry or tidying-up as opportunities for active play. Play opportunities are also provided using simple everyday resources such as a blanket, cardboard boxes, newspaper, tubes from kitchen roll, large buttons, stones or pasta to provide opportunities for creative, collaborative and extended play. Parents are also encouraged to turn off technology and to spend time with their children reading stories and enjoying books. Using the *Play Partners* method for just 10 minutes a day was found to have a positive impact on children's language development, social interactions and relationships.

A Winning Attitude course for parents

A Winning Attitude workshops are interactive and designed to give opportunities for parents and carers to discuss and share their views and opinions. Each module suggests activities for parents, carers and staff to discuss in groups rather than having a formal arrangement with a presentation by 'experts'. A key aim is for staff to be alongside parents – not lecturing them or blaming them. We need to remember that we live in a society where there is a range of cultures, beliefs and values. Differences may include:

- language;
- dress;
- food and drink;
- clothing;
- religion;
- values.

We advise those running the course to find out about the range of parents and carers that will be attending. This will promote mutual respect and help in meeting the needs of all parents and carers.

The success of the workshops is also dependent upon efficient organisation with confident leaders. Those running the course need to think about:

- informing parents and carers about the course; invitations; reply slips (try to get both parents to attend the session);
- venue and parking;
- providing a creche (to enable both parents to attend; ensure safeguarding and insurance are in place);
- layout of the room (groups rather than theatre style);
- timing;
- meet and greet;
- refreshments;
- helpers/staff attending;
- information technology required;
- production of documentation;
- feedback and follow-up to the course.

It is an obvious point, but communicating with adults is very different from communicating with children. Course leaders need to think about the key skills of communication:

- body language and position: the way we stand, use our hands, make eye contact;
- listening: it is a real skill to listen actively to others, nodding and giving signals that what they are saying is important;
- speaking clearly, thoughtfully and respectfully: the words we use and our tone of voice can change the meaning of our message.
- confidentiality: agreeing that what people share in the workshop is confidential to the group with a caveat that we all have a responsibility to pass on anything which may indicate that there is a safeguarding issue to the designated member of staff.

Teachers and practitioners have fed back to us that they appreciate having all of the resources they need to run the workshops. The resources provided for *A Winning Attitude* course include:

- PDF Workbook detailing the workshop sessions – *How to Bring out the Best in your Child*;
- eBooklet – *Parents as Play Partners*;
- PowerPoint presentation;
- video of the workshops in action;
- handout – 'The Importance of Attachment';
- e-flyer that can be adapted to promote the workshops;
- parent certificate form and parent feedback form;
- *A Winning Attitude* book (The original small book of inspirational quotes).

Although all of the materials are provided, course leaders need to familiarise themselves with the course materials in advance in order to confidently manage all of the sessions. We suggest thinking of questions that may be asked and answers that may be given (remembering that the course leaders will not have all of the answers and may need to defer to a colleague or get back to someone with the correct information). We have found that the best answers often come from parents and carers themselves who are keen to share things that have worked for them.

The sessions covered during *A Winning Attitude* course are:

- Meeting your child's emotional needs; making choices.
- Character building; code of conduct; behaviour and manners.
- Discipline: children need limits structure and consistency.
- Fun, engagement and play; building strong relationships.

The first session focuses on attachment and how parents are responsible for nurturing their children and giving them what they need. Discussion focuses on what children need emotionally in order to thrive and feel significant. The second and third sessions focus on how children develop their character, attitudes and behaviour. The key role model of the adult is discussed along with a discussion on appropriate rules, consistency and consequences. The final session focuses on parental engagement and play with particular reference to the Parents as Play Partners project (Chapter 6). The final part of the course is making a plan on how to use what has been covered during the workshops. Parents are encouraged to keep a diary for two weeks in order to share their experiences.

Conclusion

This chapter considers the role of parents and carers and whether parents need to be qualified. The Start Right Report (Ball, 1994) states that 'modern parenthood is too demanding and complex a task to be performed well merely because we

FIGURE 5.4 Play helps to deepen the relationship between adult and child

have all once been children'. Since 1994 schools and settings have mostly included parental partnership as one of their priorities. Although being involved with the school and sharing knowledge about children's development and progress is an important aspect of what Sir Christopher refers to as the *triangle of care* in the Start Right Report, we also need to include parenting and the engagement of parents with their babies and young children in what Kathy Sylva refers to as *the home learning environment* (Sammons et al., 2015). It may seem arrogant to suggest that parents need to be qualified. However, the demands of parenting are now so much more than when the report was written in 1994. We developed *A Winning Attitude* course for parents and carers to give a positive and respectful message with a forum to enable parents, carers, teachers and practitioners to address the many challenges of nurturing children and providing them with what they need in order to thrive. We believe that the course was given value by being endorsed by Cache and providing course leaders and parents with certificates. We are pleased that the course embraces the principles of *Start Right* and the current advice given by Sir Christopher including leading by example, providing children with security and protection, practising *tough love* where there is both connection and correction and working in partnership with schools and settings. We hope that this chapter, along with the others in this book, has given the reader ideas to add to Sir Christopher's guidelines for parents and will encourage a wider debate on what parents need to know. As Sir Christopher states in Chapter 1, 'early childhood is for many the turning point between success and failure in learning, work and life – which is why all children should be enabled to start right'.

References

Ball, C. (1994). *Start Right: The importance of early learning*. London: RSA.

Bowlby, J. (1988). *A secure base: clinical application of attachment theory*. London: Routledge.

Bowlby, J. (2010). *The making and breaking of affectionate bonds*. Oxon: Routledge.

Deforges, C., and Abouchaar, A. (2003). *The impact of parental involvement, parental support and family engagement on pupils' achievement and adjustment*. Nottingham: Department for Education and Skills. Report No. 433. www.dfes.go.uk/research

Field, F. (2010). *The Foundation Years: Preventing poor children becoming poor adults*. London: HM Government, p. 11.

Golding, K. (2017). *Everyday parenting with security and love*. London: Jessica Kingsley.

Hamilton-McGinty, R. (2000). *A winning attitude*. Chichester, UK: A Winning Attitude Press.

Hamilton-McGinty, R., and Preedy. P. (1917). *A parent guide to childhood issues*. www.attitudepress.com/ebooks

Hattie, J. (2008). *Visible learning: A synthesis of over 800 meta-analyses relating to achievement*. New York: Routledge.

Hughes, D. and Balylin, J. (2012). *Brain based parenting. The neuroscience of caregiving for healthy attachment*. New York. W.W. Norton & Co.

Lexmond, J. and Reeves, R. (2009). *Parents are the principal architects of a fairer society…BUILDING CHARACTER*. London: DEMOS.

Sammons, P., Toth, K., Sylva, K., Melhuish, E., Siraj, I., & Taggart, B. L. (2015). The long-term role of the home learning environment in shaping students' academic attainment in secondary school. *Journal of Children's Services*, 10(3).

Steinberg, L., Lamborn, D., Sanford, M., Dornbush, M., and Darling. N. (1992). Impact of parenting practices on adolescent achievement: Authoritative parenting, school involvement, and encouragement to succeed. *Child Development*, 63(5), 1266–1281.

6

PARENTS AS PLAY PARTNERS PROJECT

Giving children a head start through play

Pat Preedy and Kay Sanderson

Introduction

Although the Start Right Report (Ball, 1994) referred strongly to the importance of play to young children's development and learning, play versus work for children is still a widely debated topic. This chapter focuses on the development of secure attachments and schema through the *Parents as Play Partners* project conducted with a range of families in the United Arab Emirates (UAE).

Children from around the world play. Yet play is often misunderstood and disregarded as something frivolous that is not part of work. As Moyles (1989, p. 16) states: 'Play has all too often been used to infer something rather trivial and non-serious – the polar extreme to work rather than, as in a child's context, the essence of serious concentrated thinking'.

Without an understanding of the importance and power of play it is too easy to ignore it or destroy it and, in so doing, destroy childhood itself. Play is not easily definable and has presented a problem to many scholars who have tried to define and categorise it over time. Labels such as structured and unstructured play, as originally identified by Manning and Sharp (1977), and directed and free play (Moyles, 1989), do not really convey the essence and importance of play. Reflecting on these perspectives, we formulated the following key research questions:

- Do children still play? If yes, what sort of play do they engage in?
- Can the project offer parents insights into the meaning and values of play?
- Can the *play partners* method using schema-based play and low-cost natural resources assist families in developing strong attachments and engagement with their children?

Filming of the parents and children in their homes was an important part of the research design as it enabled analysis of the differences between the child's 'normal play behaviour' and of that following the introduction of activities from the *Parents as Play Partners* booklet. The findings from this study and wider implementation of the project strongly indicate that 'play' has become distorted amongst a plethora of plastic and technological devices and that the *play partners* method is an effective means of enabling parents to engage with their young children.

Parental attachment and engagement

This study particularly draws upon the research of John Bowlby – frequently considered to be the *father* of attachment theory. Bowlby believed that the earliest bonds formed by children have a tremendous impact that continues throughout life, concluding that: 'The infant and young child should experience a warm, intimate, and continuous relationship with his mother (or permanent mother substitute) in which both find satisfaction and enjoyment' (Bowlby, 1951, p. 13).

Mary Ainsworth joined Bowlby's research team in the 1950s. She was responsible for analysing James Robertson's data from a film entitled 'A Two-year-old Goes to Hospital' (Bowlby and Robertson, 1952). The film focused on the separation of children from their parents when hospitalised. Observations of children traumatised by being separated from their parents often when they were profoundly sick have had a lasting impact on our understanding of attachment. In the 1970s Ainsworth conducted her 'Strange Situation' study. In the study, researchers observed children between the ages of 12 and 18 months as they responded to a situation in which they were briefly left alone and then reunited with their mothers. Ainsworth (1978) recorded the responses of the children using the following major styles of attachment:

- secure (some distress when the caregiver leaves but is able to be comforted – secure that the caregiver will return);
- ambivalent (become very distressed when their caregiver leaves and is not able to be comforted);
- avoidant (no reaction when the caregiver leaves or arrives).

In his introduction to his father's work, Richard Bowlby highlights the importance of attachment to human development: 'Our sense of self is closely dependent on the few intimate attachment relationships we have or have had in our lives, especially our relationship with the person who raised us' (Bowlby, 2010. p. viii). It is for this reason that a key objective of the *Parents as Play Partners* project was to provide opportunities for parents and children to deepen their attachments – an important pre-requisite for a successful start to their early development and later personal, social and emotional outcomes.

Hattie (2008) defines parental engagement as setting goals together; displaying enthusiasm for learning; encouraging good study habits; asking questions; valuing experimentation, learning new things and enjoying reading. A wide body of international research consistently highlights the positive impact of parents regularly and naturally interacting and engaging with their children. Where parental engagement is strong, children have been found to experience greater success in school with higher grades, better attendance, more positive behaviour and attitudes and increased enrolment in post-secondary education. Professor Charles Desforges and Alberto Abouchaar also highlight the key impact parents have on their children: 'What parents do with their children at home through the age range, is much more significant than any other factor open to educational influence' (Desforges and Abouchaar, 2003, p. 91). Their key finding confirms that the more parents and children talk to each other about meaningful subjects, the better children achieve. Desforges' review led to the development of the 'Every Child Matters' policy Green Paper in Britain (Chief Secretary to the Treasury, 2003). The importance of parents engaging with their children has also been highlighted by Hattie (2008) in his in-depth meta-analysis of the influences on pupil learning. His 15-year analysis of 50,000 studies involving 83 million students to see what worked in education demonstrated that a combination of parental encouragement and high parental expectations were critical elements in parenting support. Hattie calculated that the effect of parental engagement over a child's school career can be equivalent to adding an extra two or three years to his or her education. The challenge for parents of young children is how to engage with their children in a way that enables sustained interactions rather than providing a space and toys for children to play away from adults or trying to 'teach' the children through adult-led activities.

The importance of play

Children around the world play even in circumstances that are extremely challenging such as war or deprivation. If children are not playing, then something is very wrong. Play rather than formal teaching supports children's huge capacity for learning. It is the natural medium through which they learn best, since it is both enjoyable and self-motivated. Play is considered to be so important for children that it is included in the UN Convention on the Rights of the Child, Article 31 (1990), which states in Article 31, part 1, p. 10 that parties recognise the right of the child to rest and leisure, to engage in play and recreational activities appropriate to the age of the child and to participate freely in cultural life and the arts.

Dr Stuart Brown, founder of *The National Institute for Play*, has interviewed thousands of people to capture their play profiles. He has also observed animal play in the wild, leading to the conclusion that play is a long-evolved behaviour important for the well-being and survival of animals. In controlled laboratory settings that limited play behaviour, animals were unable to deter aggression, or to socialise comfortably with fellow pack members. Although the linkages from these findings to humans has not been firmly established, the work of Brown (2010) is powerful in supporting the theory that children denied opportunities to play are at higher risk of presenting behaviour and social integration problems at later stages in their development.

On the surface children's play may seem to be simple. However, Hughes (2012), a leading play theorist and practitioner in the United Kingdom, suggests that there are at least 16 different play types displayed by children as they play including social, socio-dramatic, rough-and-tumble, exploratory, object, creative, communication, deep, recapitulative, symbolic, fantasy, dramatic, imaginative, locomotor, mastery and role play. Erikson (1963) highlighted the 'make-believe' element of play that enables children to learn about their social world and their cultural role within it. He gave great emphasis to play based on the recognition that young children have limited ability to communicate their problems in the way adults may. Play situations are opportunities for the child to externalise problems and to work through them and come to terms with them. Play also provides opportunities for observers to understand children's learning and development

Developing schema through play

Schema are patterns of thought or behaviour providing the basis for relating to events being experienced. During the 1970s, Chris Athey developed further the theory of schema. Athey noted how children have an interest in continually repeating an action over and over again. For example, a baby may repeatedly throw a toy from his or her high chair. Athey highlighted that these behaviours are not 'flitting' or purposeless. The child is creating schema and the role of the adult should be to 'tune in' to the child's interest and support the child to develop his or her knowledge. For example, when a toddler carries things to the adult he or she may be exploring transporting items. The adult can provide bags and trucks in order that the child can carry items in different ways. The following table summarises schema identified by Athey (2007).

TABLE 6.1 Developing schema based on the work of Chris Athey (2007)

Trajectory	Has a fascination with lines – vertical, horizontal and oblique. Repeated throwing and dropping of objects.
Rotational	Moving objects around and around. Drawing circles. Turning around.
Transporting	Moving objects or collections of objects from one place to another, perhaps using a buggy or a truck.
Enveloping and Containing	Covering things up and putting things inside. Likes posting objects and putting things in an enclosure e.g. farm animals in a field.
Transformation	Mixing paint, showing interest in melting jellies. Dressing-up.
Scattering	Emptying baskets, tipping out toys e.g. bricks, using arms and legs to scatter items, swiping objects or toys from tables.
Positioning	Placing objects in particular places e.g. lining-up cars, likes to stand in the front or back of the line.
Orientation	Explores things from different angles. Turns items over, looks behind pictures.
Connection and Separation	Interested in how things join together. Takes things apart.

Barriers to play

Play is essential for the healthy cognitive, physical, social and emotional development of children. 'Play and conversation are the main ways by which young children learn about themselves, other people and the world around them' (Ball, 1994, p. 53). The play opportunities that parents and carers provide for their children are influenced by cultural and societal norms, values and beliefs. There can be significant barriers preventing children from developing secure attachments and schema through play. In this chapter we focus on barriers associated with technology and the role of nannies/housemaids.

Technology – barrier or learning tool?

Research regarding the use of technology and the impact of the amount of screen time experienced by young children is in the early stages. The reliability and validity of the research that is available needs critical evaluation as it is frequently funded by powerful companies who produce and market the technology that is being researched.

Common Sense Media (2011) reported that approximately 72 per cent of iPad applications in the Educational Category are marketed for pre-schoolers – this is a large market that is being targeted, frequently claiming educational value for products that may be at least partly responsible for restricting children's physical movements, play and learning. The following statistics provide much food for thought:

- 60 per cent of parents do not supervise their child's technology use.
- In a typical day, children consume just over 3 hours of media. This includes computer use, cell phone use, tablet use, music and reading. Two thirds of this time is spent with *screen media* (TV, computers, the Internet, etc.) while reading is less than 20 minutes per day.
- 75 per cent of children are allowed technology in their bedrooms.

A range of research is now indicating that excessive screen time is linked to obesity, poor sleep, language delays and inattention (Sigman, 2017). Recommendations vary regarding the amount of screen time that should be allowed for children. There is a growing consensus that children under 2 years of age should not be allowed screen time at all and that children aged between 2 and 5 should be limited to no more than an hour a day in total. This information highlights the importance of managing and monitoring technology use by our young children. We need to ask ourselves:

- What learning opportunities are being provided?
- Is time spent on devices at the expense of active and creative play that enables children to develop schema, attachments and social skills?

There are some positive studies published citing the benefits of hand-held devices in developing literacy skills for children experiencing disability (Flewitt, Kucirkova,

& Messer, 2014). However, where technology use is found to be beneficial, this is frequently linked to adult support and interactions with the child rather than the child engaging with technology in isolation.

Nannies/housemaids – support or barrier?

In the Gulf Region (the location of this study), many local and expatriate families employ housemaids and nannies to help with childcare and life in the family home. Many parents do not have extended families to call upon for help and are left with no alternative but to employ housemaids/nannies.

Most of the female workers employed as housemaids and nannies originate from Sri Lanka, Philippines, India and African sub-continent. They usually live in the family home or in an adjacent maid's room and many work long hours for little money. The majority are untrained and unqualified, lacking the experience, skills and knowledge to meet the physical and emotional needs of babies and young children. All too often electronic hand-held devices and the television are used to keep children occupied. Research is limited in this area, but research published in the *Journal of Childhood Research* conducted in 2005 on housemaids and nannies indicated that 58 per cent of children under the age of 3 in the region spend on average between 30 to 70 hours a week with housemaids and nannies. The report stated that although not always a positive or enriching experience, there was an economic benefit to parents using their domestic help as child care. 'A maid is a very economical alternative and provides a long list of additional services' (Roumani, 2005, p. 8).

As many children are spending large amounts of time with housemaids/nannies we wanted to provide parents with an easy method of engaging with their children rather than leaving childcare almost completely to the maid or nanny. We introduced parents to the 'ten-minute rule' limiting the time expected for each *play partners* session to 10 minutes – providing a little of the right input every day can have a huge impact. In reality, once parents experienced the benefits of playing with their children as play partners they extended the time allocation, encouraging their nannies and housemaids to also adopt the method. Although the focus of this research project is supporting parents in using the *play partners* method, it is intended to expand the project as part of training for nannies and housemaids in the region.

The *Parents as Play Partners* project

The project focused on four families who had all been residents within the UAE for many years. All of the children in the study attended nursery school. Two of the sample group had an older sibling. All parents involved in the study worked and had assistance with childcare within the home. Each of the families involved had volunteered independently of each other. As highlighted by Babbie (2001), purposive sampling was ideal in this situation as we needed to reach a targeted sample quickly and sampling for proportionality was not the main concern of the researchers. Volunteer sampling, as outlined by Black (1999), can be an inexpensive way of

TABLE 6.2 Participant details

Nationality of family	Child's age	Parental involvement	Siblings	Environment	Location
Greek	2 years 1 month	Both	No	Apartment	Dubai
Egyptian	2 years 6 months	Both	Yes – older brother	Villa	Dubai
British	2 years	Both	Yes – older brother	Villa	Dubai
Nigerian	2 years 4 months	Both	No	Bedsit	Dubai

ensuring sufficient numbers for a study, but can be highly unrepresentative. Taking this into account, families from different nationalities and socio-economic groups were selected to provide a more balanced representation.

The families who volunteered to take part in the study did so for various reasons including:

- to improve the communication of their child;
- to change some unruly behaviours and attitudes of their child;
- to strengthen the attachment between themselves and their child;
- to develop engagement and play skills between themselves and their child.

Research design

We designed a booklet for parents in electronic form and hard copy detailing the importance of play and the *play partners* method, including how to use everyday activities and natural resources to engage with their child through play. The key tools used throughout this study were filming and observation. It was agreed that all filming would be completed in the children's home environment to enable families, especially those with younger children, to feel comfortable during the play sessions. To manage this effectively it was vitally important that parents understood the important role they needed to play in ensuring that the child is comfortable and that they understood the research process, as outlined in the NCB guidelines on research with young children (Shaw, Brady and Davey, 2011, p. 19).

As the study involved young children, consent forms had to be completed by parents not only for the home visits and research undertaken but also for the filming and editing of footage gained. Although none of the research was undertaken in the UK, the UAE has limited guidance on research with children, so the guidelines set by BERA (2004) were adhered to in order to ensure that the best interest and rights of the child were of primary consideration.

Although informed consent was gained, the researchers used the term 'provisional consent', as no one could predict how the children would react in front of the cameras or whether they would want to play at all with so many extra, strange people in their domain. This provisional consent is on-going and dependent on the relationships of trust and collaboration built up between the participants and the researcher team. Flewitt (2005, p. 4) and Simons and Usher (2000) describe this provisional consent as *negotiated in situated contexts on a minute-by-minute basis.*

Home visits were scheduled with each family allowing a day for each visit. It was important to enter each home respectfully allowing time to build the relationship as it was uncertain how each child would react when the researchers and two film crew arrived. The researchers were keen that the families felt relaxed and not rushed whilst in the flow of filming.

An important aspect of the research was to share with parents the key underpinning theories to the research – attachment, engagement and developing schematic play using the *Parents as Play Partners* booklet. The sections covered in the booklet were the importance of play; parents as play partners; using everyday activities as play opportunities; providing play opportunities at home and being active together. To ascertain the impact of the intervention parents would keep a diary for two weeks following the home visit. There would also be an interview with parents and a post-questionnaire to glean valuable insights into their experiences.

The method

Initial pre-questionnaires were given to families to obtain general information about the family unit and to determine the interpretation of play by parents. Whilst the parents were completing these the film crew set up the equipment ready for filming and the research team positioned themselves out of sight, so as not to distract the child and parents in play. The same procedure was replicated in each family home, so that the same amount of footage would be generated.

Families were asked to play with their child as they would normally do, using any toys and materials that the child was used to playing with. This activity lasted for 15 minutes, which gave them 5 minutes to settle into an activity and 10 minutes to play. No guidance was given to the child or the parents in terms of what to play and how to play, so communication, engagement and attachment were all under the control of the child and the parents.

Following this filming one of the parents was taken aside and the *Parents as Play Partners* booklet was explained to them (20–30 minutes) and the activities that would form the intervention. Whilst this was taking place, the other parent was asked to distract the child, so that all plastic and technological items could be removed from the play area being filmed. These toys and games were replaced with a selection of household objects and items and materials found naturally in the home, for example pans, spoons, socks, baskets, cushions, throws and dried food items such as pasta and beans. In addition, all technology was removed from the play area – all mobile devices had to be turned off and hidden and televisions turned off.

The second round of filming took place for another 10 minutes. The play on this occasion was to be led by the child, with the parent communicating, joining-in

FIGURE 6.1 Commercial toys can create barriers to play

the play and offering encouragement – at no time were they to take the lead. Types of play activity included dinners being made, dens being built, food being created, washing being emptied, hide and seek within boxes and reading in tents made from throws over table and chairs.

Following the filming parents were given guidance as to what to include in their diaries or blogs, depending on which they chose to keep. A date was agreed for the collection of the diaries, interview and post-questionnaire. This marked the end of the study for these parents and children.

Findings

Pre-questionnaire

The pre-questionnaire specifically focused on what was understood by play, how important the parents thought it was, and what the children regularly played with and enjoyed.

Interestingly none of the respondents mentioned home-made learning materials or activities and materials centred round what is available at home or in the garden. During the home visit parents were asked to play with their child as they would normally do. The play areas were crowded with plastic toys both big and small, TV, musical instruments, books and a variety of toys and games. The following was observed:

- analysis of the children's body language revealed high levels of frustration and anxiety, play was individual although parents were present;

FIGURE 6.2 Playing with your child as a play partner deepens and extends play and learning

TABLE 6.3 Responses to the pre-questionnaire

What do you understand by play?	All answers referred to children using play as part of their development and learning – particularly language development.
How important do you think it is for children to play?	All agreed it was very important.
What sort of play does your child engage in?	All responses involved toys, balls, cars and anything available.
Who is involved in your child's play?	This had a mixed response: nursery staff, nanny, friends, teachers, mother and father.
What does your child enjoy playing with?	Commercial toys/media.

- concentration was limited – children drifted from toy to game to book to toy, no sustained play took place;
- anxiety showed on parents' and children's faces, tantrums started, and aggressive behaviour was displayed, hitting with cars and throwing toys;
- parents tried to control situations and to offer another toy to replace the one thrown, the same action occurred again and again;
- all four children were in tears, showing aggression by the end of the 10 minutes with parents looking exhausted and frustrated.

FIGURE 6.3 Commercial toys can be limiting, leading to frustration and aggression

Intervention – introduction of Play Partners module

Following the first 10 minutes of filming, the *Parents as Play Partners* booklet was introduced to the parents and materials from around the home were positioned in the play area for the child to lead the play with parents following, interacting and engaging.

Key findings – play-based activities after intervention

Children and parents appeared to quickly forget the presence of cameras and became immersed in the joint activity. The analysis of the footage after the intervention and research tool had been introduced was very different from the earlier filming:

- analysis of the children's body language revealed high levels of engagement and involvement in the play with their parents post intervention;
- noticeably, children turned their trunk towards parents and a close triangle was formed between parents, object (of play) and child;
- typically, their body movements became more purposeful suggesting a greater depth of interest and involvement in the activity;
- notably, in terms of 'flow and immersion in the moment' (Harding, 2014) all children exhibited signs of deep play – wallowing in play (Bruce, 1996) in close proximity to their parents;
- frequently, footage clearly revealed the compelling nature of schema development, for example through the simplicity of resources such as a blanket to form a den (enclosure schema). Many other schemas were also in evidence: trajectory, enveloping, transforming, transporting;
- increased frequency of moments of spontaneous laughter from parents and children.

The change in the quality of engagement and the relationship between parents and children were striking after the intervention. Through play, parents and children could engage for sustained periods of time in a relaxed and meaningful way.

FIGURES 6.4 AND 6.5   Being a play partner and using everyday items enables children and parents to engage and become immersed in the play

TABLE 6.4 Q5 How has the project impacted?

	Family 1	Family 2	Family 3	Family 4
Yourself	It has helped me to consciously create more time for play with my son and help him learn every day.	Very positively, new ideas, approaches. Happy to make something more creative, happy to see our son being more creatively and constructively entertained.	I want to change a bit of my day to be more involved in playing.	I feel less tired and stressed. I make time to play and read and life is better, I have my maid read also, things are better. I can now spend time with my younger son.
Your child	It has helped our son to play more and be confident to try new things and to play with other kids nicely and share.	Very positively. He can now engage with us more effectively and us with him. There is a better sense of continuity between home and pre-school.	He is so happy, he loves his new den and his sock puppets and bath times are so much fun with the kitchen utensils.	He is talking so much more and is not aggressive any more. The school is happy with him inshallah.
Your spouse	It has helped him learn how to play more and create time for our son.	Very positive, quality time spent as a family instead of one on one.	Very happy, he has made dens in the bedroom and now they read every night together, it is wonderful!	He now plays with our children as he has ideas. They make paper aeroplanes and models together.
Your family	We all had fun playing together and it helped us to come up with new ideas and things to do every day.	Very positively, quality time is spent together, more creativity, more enjoyable, more productive, created some time for togetherness.	We are happy and thank God that we found you. Our home is a full of paintings and we have less and less tantrums.	It was an amazing experience for our little family. Thank you for enlightening us through it. We definitely have a different perspective to playing now!

Although filming was stopped after the allocated time, the children and parents were so engaged in a state of play that they continued, oblivious that filming had ceased.

Post-intervention questionnaires and interviews

The post-questionnaire focused predominantly on the *Parents as Play Partners* module and the project itself. The first four questions related to the ease of use of the module and if it was understandable. All agreed that the module had been easy to use and understand. A key question, which the researchers were interested to review, concerned the impact of the module and the answers are outlined in Table 6.4.

The final two questions concerned the continued use of the *Parents as Play Partners* module and the recommendation of it to others, as this was of interest in terms of future research. Responses can be seen in Table 6.5.

Key findings – Drawings and materials made by the children and diary entries

The drawings and materials made by the children were extremely creative. The children had used their imaginations to make sock puppets, wooden spoon people, football fields made from straws and corks and cotton wool. In addition, food had been chopped and washing emptied from machines, dens had been erected and sieves used in the bath. The diary entries were equally impressive, and a few entries have been listed below:

- 19.11.2014 – He loves reading the book with the penguin travelling in an umbrella, so we thought it would be a great idea to make an umbrella today. We started off for an umbrella, but, along the way he decided to create a hat

TABLE 6.5 – Q6 and Q7

Q6. Will you continue to use any aspects of the project? If yes, why?	Q7. Would you recommend *Parents as Play Partners* to friends with children? If yes, why?
Yes, it brings us closer to our kids.	Yes.
Yes, it is a most constructive way of spending time together and he is so much happier.	Yes, same as for Q6.
Absolutely! It's a great project for parents. It will definitely help us to continue to create time and have fun together as we watch our son grow up.	Parents sometimes run out of ideas of what to do with their kids. I think this module will come in handy as it has useful tips for everyone.
Yes, because we now all play together for the first time, no one is left out and our son is getting more confident.	Yes, because it is excellent!

instead. We then played the game to keep the hat on our heads for as long as possible, this was really good fun!!!

- 14.11.2014 – Today daddy and me played let's cook dinner together. I learnt how to use the knife and I chopped up the vegetables. Our little chef in the making, amazing!
- 10.11.2014 – We made a den from an old curtain. My son didn't want me to go out of it! He loved spending time with me in there even if we are just sitting doing nothing! But as a change it is the only place he lets me hold a book to read it for him for more than two minutes!!
- 11.11.2014 – Dressing up, both my boys (6 and 2.6) wore my high heel shoes and baby blankets as capes to pretend to be Elsa with ice paws from Frozen! Yes boys like Frozen movie too. My little one came to say a lot of new words as he played pretending, examples; ice, here I am, anyway, let it go, was so much fun, we laughed lots.
- 14.11.14 – We had a beautiful day today. The weather was perfect and we spend the whole day outdoors strolling around the city. The beautiful day was complete with my son and his dad playing puppet socks in the bath, he loves them and talks so much when using them!

Discussion

Bowlby and Ainsworth demonstrated that nurturing and responding are the primary determinants of attachment. Desforges and Abouchaar (2003) and Hattie (2008) went on to link parental engagement to a child's later success. The challenge for parents is how to remove barriers enabling them to engage with their children within what is often a busy and challenging life. Research on the importance of schema-based play by Athey (2007) and Brown (2010) highlights that play is a natural method for engaging with children, for developing secure attachments and enhancing conceptual development – the roots of lifelong learning. The *Parents as Play Partners* project gives parents an easy-to-use tool that is inexpensive and not time-consuming. Becoming play partners enables them to engage with their children rather than being a supervisor or instructor. They are able to tune-in to their children's interests and extend them, deepening the relationship as well as enhancing the child's physical and cognitive development.

This deep understanding of the complexity of children's play was essential in the development of the *Play Partners* method. The film footage taken during the play sessions clearly highlights how both the children and their parents naturally move between the different types of play, provided there are opportunities for them to be imaginative and creative with a range of natural and everyday materials.

The pre- and post-intervention filming highlighted how the children and parents became relaxed, involved, engaged and in a state of flow once the parent assumed the role of *play partner* (Csikszentimihalyi, 1991; Laevers, 1994). When the children were leading the play, they were fully engaged, and the closeness and attachment between parent and child could be observed. The children and parents

FIGURE 6.6   Being a play partner is fun for the parent and the child

were so immersed in playing that filming had stopped, the equipment had been packed away and the researchers and film crew were just sat observing until one of the parents realised we had finished.

Conclusion

A key aim of the *Parents as Play Partners* project was to enable both parents and children to develop secure attachments that will be instrumental in providing support and a positive start to school and the beginning of lifelong education. A small sample size was important to use in the initial study as this enabled the researchers to refine the method and the module for future implementation. Initial findings are extremely encouraging. It was possible to share with parents wide-ranging and complex research with regards to attachment, engagement and schema-based play. They were able to understand quickly the *Play Partners* module and to immediately build upon it after the research team had left, as detailed in the post interviews and questionnaires.

When children start school, they need to be confident in themselves, have good communication skills and be receptive to learning. Through play, parents can be instrumental in supporting their children in developing the skills and attributes necessary to go forward to enjoy and experience learning to their fullest potential.

Following on from the success of the pilot study, the *Parents as Play Partners* findings were shared at the BSME (British Schools of the Middle East) conference in Qatar 2016. The project has been extended through workshops organised by schools within the UAE and is now available free to schools who register at www.playpartnersproject.co.uk and as part of *A Winning Attitude* course for parents (Chapter 5).

A natural extension of the project would be to measure the impact of the intervention when children enter school and are baseline assessed.

References

Ainsworth, M. D. S. (1978). *Patterns of Attachment: A Psychological Study of the Strange Situation.* Hillsdale, NJ: Lawrence Erlbaum Associates.

Arnold, C. & The Pea Green Team. (2010). *Understanding Schemas and Emotion in Early Childhood.* London: Sage.

Athey, C. (2007). *Extending Thought in Young Children: A Parent Teacher Partnership.* New York: Sage.

Babbie, E. (2001). *The Practice of Social Research* (9th edn). Belmont, CA: Wadsworth Thomson.

Ball, C. (1994). *Start Right, The Importance of Early Learning.* London: RSA.

Bowlby, J. & Robertson, J. (1952). [Film] *A Two-year-old Goes to Hospital. A Scientific Film.* Robertson Films.

Black, T. R. (1999). *Doing Quantitative Research in the Social Sciences: An Integrated Approach to Research Design, Measurement, and Statistics.* Thousand Oaks, CA: Sage.

Bowlby, J. (1951). *Maternal Care and Mental Health.* World Health Organization Monograph (Serial No. 2).

Bowlby, J. (2010). *The Making and Breaking of Affectionate Bonds.* Oxon: Routledge.

Bretherton, I. (1992). The origins of attachment theory: John Bowlby and Mary Ainsworth. *Developmental Psychology,* 28, 759–775.

British Educational Research Association (BERA) (2004). *Revised Ethical Guidelines for Educational Research.* Cheshire: BERA.

Brown, S. (2010). *Play: How it Shapes the Brain, Opens the Imagination and Invigorates the Soul.* London: Penguin.

Bruce. T. (1996). *Helping Young Children to Play.* London: Hodder and Stoughton.

Common Sense Media (2011). www.commonsensemedia.org

Csikszentmihalyi, M. (1991). *Flow: The Psychology of Optimal Experience.* London: Harper Collins.

Cocozza, P. (2014, January 8). Are iPads and tablets bad for young children? *The Guardian.* Retrieved from, http:www.theguardian.com

Desforges, C. & Abouchaar, A. (2003). *The Impact of Parental Involvement, Parental Support and Family Engagement on Pupils Achievement and Adjustment.* Nottingham: Department for Education and Skills. Report No. 433. www.dfes.go.uk/research

Erikson, E. (1963). *Childhood and Society.* New York: W.W. Norton and Company.

Flewitt, R. (2005). Conducting research with young children: Some ethical considerations. *Early Child Development and Care,* 175(6), 553–565.

Flewitt, R., Kucirkova, N. & Messer, D. (2014). Touching the virtual; touching the real: iPads and enabling literacy for students experiencing disability. *Australian Journal of Language and Literacy,* 37(2), 107–116.

Harding, J. (2014). The Institute of Maternal and Child Health (and wellbeing). Retrieved from https://prezi.com/-nv99m11kqca/the-institute-of-maternal-and-child-health-and-wellbeing/

Hattie, J. (2008). *Visible Learning: A Synthesis of Over 800 Meta-Analyses Relating to Achievement*. Oxon: Routledge.

Hughes, B. (2012). *Evolutionary Playwork*. London: Routledge.

Laevers, F. (1994). *The Innovative Project Experiential Education and the Definition of Quality in Education*. Studia Pedagogica Belgium: Leuven University Press.

Louis, S. & Feathersone, S. (2008). *Understanding Schema in Young Children. Again! And Again!* Norfolk: Fakenham Prepress Solutions.

Manning, K., & Sharp, A. (1977). *Structuring Play in the Early Years at School*. London: Ward Lock. Moyles, J. ([1989]2013). *Play and Early Years: Birth-to-Seven-Years*. Cardiff: Play Wales.

Roumani, H. B. (2005). A study of the use of housemaids as nannies, as opposed to qualified child care givers, in households in the Arabian Gulf. *Journal of Early Childhood Research*, 3(2), 149–167.

Shaw, C., Brady, L. C. & Davey, C. (2011). Guidelines for Research with Children and Young People. London: NCB Research Centre. National Children's Bureau. Registered charity number: 258825.

Sigman, A. (2017). *Screen Dependency Disorders: a new challenge for child neurology*. JICNA. ISSN 2410–6410. Available at: http://jicna.org/index.php/journal/article/view/67.

Simons, H. & Usher, R. (2000). *Situated Ethics in Educational Research*. London: Routledge.

The Treasury Department. (2003). *Every Child Matters*, Government Green Paper. London: The Stationery Office (Id 153606).

7

EXECUTIVE FUNCTIONS

Skills that underpin success

Karen Morris

Introduction

The social class achievement gap remains one of the most entrenched and challenging problems in the UK educational system, despite the introduction of the Early Years Foundation Stage (EYFS) (DfES, 2007; DfE, 2012, 2014). The Education Endowment Foundation reports that the 21 per cent of children eligible for free school meals (a proxy indicator of social class) start school lagging behind their peers and that the gap widens as they progress through the education system. The government's introduction of the Pupil Premium (April 2011) and the Early Years Pupil Premium (April 2015) is a response to this attainment gap and an attempt to address it by giving settings and schools additional targeted funds. Recent data (Andrews, Robinson, & Hutchinson, 2017, p. 40) indicate a slight lessening of the gap since 2007 for disadvantaged pupils (those eligible for the Pupil Premium) but note that *on the current trend, it will take a staggering 50 years before the gap is closed and disadvantaged pupils finally achieve parity with their more affluent peers.* A powerful reason for re-defining early childhood education.

This chapter focuses on an important set of skills that hold out some promise for helping close the gap but that are not explicitly covered in the EYFS. These skills are called executive functions – they are sometimes also referred to as the skills of self-regulation. They are skills that underpin effective social and emotional engagement and successful cognitive development – these strands of development both draw on the prefrontal cortex and are much more intertwined than courses on child development tend to imply. The chapter begins by outlining what is meant by 'executive functions'. Consideration will then be given to the evidence that targeting these skills in the Early Years can help close the social class achievement gap. Finally, taking a holistic view of development, the chapter will indicate how practitioners can hone their recognition, scaffolding and challenge of children's executive function skills through a wide range of developmentally appropriate activities and practices. Executive functions run through all the purposeful activities young children engage in. Advocating executive function intervention is not to suggest that additional content be added to the curriculum: it is to highlight the potential for closing the gap of an informed and expert practitioner who explicitly scaffolds and extends the executive functions involved in children's day-to-day activities.

What are executive functions?

Executive functions are a set of skills that enable us to carry out (execute) tasks in a purposeful way. While the term may be new to many readers, they will soon realise that executive functions comprise skills that effective parents and practitioners have always promoted and valued. People of all ages depend on their executive functions, as illustrated in the following scenario.

Think of practitioners working with a group of 3–5-year-olds. The practitioners have planned a play session where the children listen to a story about a teddy bears' picnic and then have access to the soft toys and some new tea sets. As they observe the children, the practitioners are noting any actions or language that represent evidence of developmental progress. The practitioners are particularly aware of one child who has recently seen a Speech and Language Therapist who advised that the child requires processing time for understanding and responding to language. One practitioner, although quick to understand what the child is trying to say, takes care to wait patiently and allow the child the extra time he requires to formulate what he wants to say. The play of the large majority of children does not develop in the expected direction of a teddy bears' picnic. Instead they run around the garden with cups and saucers, trying to keep the cups on the saucers and laughing when they fall off. One practitioner watches for a while and then suggests to some children that they might try large plates instead of saucers. Another suggests that some children might like to try putting a little water in the cups. Below we shall see how this brief scenario illustrates practitioners drawing significantly on executive skills.

Executive functions are generally broken into three main categories: working memory; inhibition; and cognitive flexibility (also known as *attention shifting*) (Diamond & Lee, 2011; Garon, Bryson, & Smith, 2008). Working memory refers to the ability to hold several things in mind *working* with them simultaneously. Inhibition is to do with holding back impulses, avoiding distractions and keeping focus. Cognitive flexibility is required to change and develop plans. We all use our executive functions continuously to navigate life.

Executive functions and the lifespan

Executive functions are important throughout the lifespan. There is a spurt in executive function development in the early years, particularly between the ages of 3–6 years and, to a lesser extent, in adolescence. The preschool executive function developmental spurt points to the importance of explicit targeting of these foundational skills by edu-cationalists aiming to prevent the social class gap. Executive functions peak in young adulthood and decline thereafter (Best & Miller, 2010). At any age, executive functions are negatively impacted by tiredness, lack of sleep, stress and loneliness (Diamond, 2015). Many adults will be able to relate to the increased incidence of forgetting things or, for example, losing the car keys when under stress. Practitioners will often tend to take their excellent executive functions for granted but when exhausted will become aware of how effortful it is to work with young children. For young children, it is vitally important for optimum development of their executive functions that both their physical needs (including sufficient sleep) and their psychological needs are met. The latter comprise the needs for relatedness (attachment/belonging – see Chapter 6); competence (exploring through play – also in Chapter 6); and autonomy (becoming themselves) (Deci & Ryan, 2000; Morris, 2015).

Executive functions and the brain

Successful executive functioning is the behavioural manifestation of brain develop-ment. Executive functions are associated with the prefrontal cortex. This part of the brain is particularly sensitive to stress (Diamond, 2015): enabling optimal executive function development can therefore be added to all the other good reasons for providing children with stable, nurturing environments. The connections in the prefrontal cortex increase significantly in 3–5-year-olds. It is crucially important that children at risk of poor outcomes are offered environments and opportunities that promote the development of the connections within the prefrontal cortex and between the prefrontal cortex and other parts of the brain. A focus on executive functions may achieve this.

Executive functions are often portrayed as 'top down' (brain driven) processes (Zelazo & Carlson, 2012). While the role of the prefrontal cortex in the brain is well-established as crucial for executive functions (Center on the Developing Child Harvard University, 2011; Diamond, 2011; Garon et al., 2008), some researchers now also acknowledge that 'bottom up' motor processes also play a role in their early development (Shaheen, 2013). This points to a key role for movement in the development of executive functions in early childhood education (see Chapters 3 and 4 of this book).

Executive functions in young children

Let us look briefly at the three strands of executive functions in young children. Executive functions allow children to move beyond merely reacting to the environ-ment with their attention being grabbed by any sight or sound. Executive functions are effortful and enable planned, purposeful activity and meaningful engagement. Children whose executive functions are not at age-typical levels should be seen as needing support to develop these skills rather than as presenting 'behaviour' problems.

The three elements of executive have different developmental trajectories, with working memory appearing first, followed by inhibition and then cognitive flexibility. The burst in development that begins at about 3 years of age is thought to reflect the increasing integration of the three elements (Garon et al., 2008).

Working memory

Working memory refers to remembering things and mentally manipulating them – not just remembering parrot-fashion but, for example, ordering items or making connections between items and linking to previous experience. We see evidence of young children's working memory developing when, for example, they follow instructions of increasing length and in the correct order. Other examples of working memory in action include making sense of a story or recognising similarities between objects. Drawing on experience uses working memory and is enhanced by reflecting on (talking through) experiences.

Success in the 'pairs' game often enjoyed by children depends on working memory. Picture cards are set out with the face down and each player turns over two cards at a time. The aim is to find matching pairs, which can then be removed, giving the player a further 'go'. Similarly, Kim's game, where players see a tray of objects and then have to work out which have been removed, calls on working memory.

An example of a test of working memory for young children is one where the child hears a string of words and has to repeat them backwards (e.g. hears 'cat, dog, sheep', says 'sheep, dog, cat'). The more words a child can correctly reverse in this way, the stronger the working memory.

Inhibition

Inhibition is to do with controlling impulses, avoiding distractions and delaying gratification. When young children wait their turn, stand in line, share toys or maintain attention in the face of distractions, they are exercising this executive function. Learning to pause and think when working out problems, rather than impetuously doing or saying the first thing that comes to mind, is an important part of inhibition.

Mischel's famous 'marshmallow test' taps inhibition (Mischel, Shoda, & Rodriguez, 1989). Children sit with one marshmallow placed in front of them and are told they can eat it now, or they can wait and have two marshmallows in a little while. Interestingly, longitudinal studies have shown that the young children in Mischel's original experiments who were able to wait for two marshmallows have tended as adults to have better long-term outcomes (employment, health and wellbeing) than the children who did not manage to wait (Mischel, 2014). This points to the long-term significance of executive functions.

Cognitive flexibility/attention shifting

Young children who take roles in play, modifying their language and actions to the role, are showing cognitive flexibility. This executive function is also being used when children are able to change their approach to a 'problem' (be it a construction task or an attempt to make friends) when their initial strategy does not deliver the desired outcome.

A common test of children's cognitive flexibility is a card sorting task where first they have to sort cards on the basis of, for example, colour but then they are asked to sort by another dimension such as shape.

Practitioners will often be aware of children whose executive function development is less advanced than their peers'. A delay in the development of inhibition is especially noticeable – these are the children who flit from activity to activity, have difficulty sharing and waiting and are often viewed as presenting behavioural problems (although recognising their difficulties as a lack of executive functions and a consequent need for 'opportunities and support to practise skills such as paying attention, waiting and managing impulses' (Morris, 2015, p. 112) is a more constructive way of framing these behaviours).

Evidence of a social class gap in executive functions in the early years

Hackman and Farah (2009) review studies suggesting a strong link between low socioeconomic status and poorer development of executive functions. The Dunedin study (Moffitt et al., 2011), which followed 1,034 children from birth to age 34, found that children with more developed executive functions were more likely to come from higher socioeconomic groups. This longitudinal study found that 'a gradient of childhood self-control' predicted many important outcomes relating to health and achievement at age 34. Moreover, children who moved up the self-control rankings over time (those whose rate of progress enabled them to 'overtake' others) had the positive outcomes consistent with their improved ranking and not their original ranking. McClelland is amongst researchers claiming early executive function predicts educational success more than any other factor (McClelland & Wanless, 2012).

While it is not known why there is a gap in executive functions between social classes, it may be, at least in part, from the pressures imposed on families by poverty (Raver & Blair, 2016). When parents' energy is sapped by daily struggles to feed and shelter themselves and their children, the consequence may be that parents neither model effective executive functioning nor provide optimal opportunities for children to practise these skills. Factors that impede executive function development are many, and include: stressful living conditions; lack of sleep; limited opportunities for free movement (undue restraint in car seat or similar, being mostly indoors in cramped space); rarely experiencing focussed attention (television constantly on, adults frequently diverted by phone etc); erratic discipline; few opportunities for imaginative play with other children. It is, however, essential to remember that while aggregated data indicates a social class gap, not every child from a poor family will have poorly developed executive functions and, conversely, not every child from the higher socioeconomic classes will have well-developed executive functions. Nor are child-rearing practices the only factor involved in executive function development – innate individual differences also play a role (Miyake & Friedman, 2012).

Targeting executive functions to 'close the gap'

The Education Endowment Fund [online] aims to provide evidence to guide effective use of the Early Years Premium to close the gap. It concludes that executive function (self-regulation) interventions offer 'high impact for very low cost, based on limited evidence'. The Education Endowment Fund seeks high quality, consistent evidence that is often a challenge in the real world of education initiatives where factors cannot be controlled to the same extent as in a scientific laboratory. Evidence continues to be gathered (e.g. Steenebergen, Olszewski-Kubilius, & Calvert, 2015) and Adele Diamond, a leading authority in the field, argues that research funding bodies should broaden the areas of executive function research they are willing to consider [online]. It is promising that a number of the studies looking at the impact of executive function interventions find that they do make a positive difference, and particularly (sometimes exclusively) for children from poorer backgrounds. This suggests their potential importance in helping close the gap.

To harness the full power of executive function intervention for closing the gap, it is important for practitioners to become adept at recognising how executive functions are involved in all activities and to continuously scaffold and extend children's use of them. Many different approaches can boost executive functions in the Early Years (Diamond & Lee, 2011; Diamond, 2010, 2012) and some will be outlined below. The wide variety of approaches associated with improving young children's executive functions offers both advantages and challenges to those aiming to close the gap. The advantages include the fact that it is not necessary to find time to add new content to the curriculum: executive function development can take place through the activities children are already engaging in and the opportunities for developing them are multiple. A cross-curricular approach is also more likely to cater for individual preferences. Children differ in the activities that attract and energise them and, if executive functions are enhanced throughout the curriculum, it follows that the support will be provided in children's favoured activities where they are likely to perform to their best. It can, however, be challenging to ensure that executive function development remains centre-stage when it is more than a case of implementing a set package to boost executive functions. To provide children with the best opportunities for executive function development, they need to keep practising tasks that use them and 'the bar' needs to be consistently raised (Diamond & Ling, 2016). Children also need to practise the various components of executive functions across a range of contexts since specific programmes tend to be narrow in their effects rather than generalising across types of activities (Diamond & Ling, 2016).

Tools of the Mind curriculum

The curriculum that is probably most associated with executive function development is the Tools of the Mind curriculum ('Tools') (Bodrova & Leong, 2007), which is an early education programme developed from Vygotskian theory and used in parts of the United States. It is widely regarded as embedding executive functions throughout the curriculum, in addition to placing an explicit focus on executive function development (Bodrova, Leong, & Akhutina, 2011; Diamond, 2011). Let us look at some of the evidence for the effectiveness of the 'Tools' curriculum.

Adele Diamond is a Canadian researcher who argues strongly for the pivotal role of executive functions in children's outcomes. In 2007 she was presented with an unusual and valuable opportunity to evaluate the effectiveness of the 'Tools' curriculum in closing the gap (Diamond, Barnett, Thomas, & Munro, 2007). A school district in the United States was opening new preschools for 3–4-year-olds from low-income families and invited Diamond's research team to run a research project in which classrooms were randomly allocated to run either 'Tools' or a 'balanced literacy' curriculum. Children in both programmes were similar in age, ethnicity, family income and educational level. All the teachers were newly recruited receiving equal amounts of training on the approach they were required to deliver.

Towards the end of the second year, the children were tested on a series of executive function tasks, which were novel activities for both groups. The children in 'Tools' performed significantly better on demanding executive function tasks than the 'balanced literacy' children. Indeed, although all of the preschools had committed to running the allocated programmes for 2 years, one preschool with both a 'Tools' and a 'balanced literacy' class deemed it unethical to deprive children of the benefits it detected with 'Tools' and so delivered 'Tools' to all the children in the second year. The positive effects the 'Tools' curriculum appeared to have on executive functions have been replicated in other studies, including one by Blair and Raver (2014). Of particular relevance for closing the gap, the latter study found that 'Tools' appeared to be more effective in classrooms with high poverty indices (i.e. those where the gap would be expected to be largest). It is beyond the scope of this chapter to fully explain the 'Tools' curriculum, which has its roots in Vygotskian theory. It is discussed here as a strong example of how focussing on executive functions might help close the gap. Readers wishing for a full understanding of Tools of the Mind are directed to the book of the same name by Bodrova and Leong (2007).

Research-informed ideas for developing children's executive functions

The ideal is that practitioners develop the ability to identify, scaffold and challenge children's executive functions throughout their activities. In the section below, some activities and strategies that emerge from the research are outlined to provide specific examples of executive function intervention in practice. These are intended as pointers to guide a cross-curricular approach rather than as a definitive programme.

Physical movement and executive functions in young children

Physical activities that make increasing demands for self-control, such as those described in Chapter 4 as part of the *Movement for Learning* project, and traditional martial arts, benefit executive functions (Diamond & Lee, 2011). So too can a range of action games familiar to many practitioners. Games like 'Simon Says' and musical statues help children develop the ability to inhibit physical movement on cue. Other such games can promote cognitive flexibility (one clap means 'stand still'; two claps mean 'go'; and then vice versa) and working memory (if there is an 'S' in your name, run to the other side of the room; if you have a little brother, sit down). The demands of such games can be easily reduced or increased to provide scaffolding or challenge, as appropriate.

Two high-quality, recent studies using these types of games suggest benefits to the children whose executive functions were initially at the lowest levels (Schmitt, McClelland, Tominey, & Acock, 2015; Tominey & McClelland, 2011). Practising these types of games can contribute towards closing the gap.

Pretend play

Play where children adopt roles has a strong theoretical basis as a key vehicle for executive function development in early childhood. Vygotsky (1896–1934) stressed the importance of 'higher mental functions' or mental tools and his followers, including the originators of the 'Tools' curriculum, note the close similarity between Vygotskian theoretical concepts and the more recent empirical work on executive functions (Bodrova et al., 2011). In Vygotskian theory, imaginative, make-believe play is the 'leading activity' for preschoolers – in other words, the activity they are predisposed to engage in and to benefit from the most. Vygotsky (1978, p. 99) remarked that 'a child's greatest self-control occurs in play'. The example is often quoted of children who only manage to stand still for a tiny amount of time when requested to do so by an adult but who manage to stand stock still for much longer when they choose a play role that demands this (e.g. sentry guard).

Both 'Tools' and the EYFS espouse a play-based pedagogy but the two are different in practice. In a classroom using 'Tools' children are involved in planning their play and carrying through their plans in a way that is unusual in EYFS-based practice. Practitioners in 'Tools' classrooms are expected to promote increasingly mature play by, for example: modelling imaginative rather than literal use of objects in play and providing props that lend themselves to multiple imaginative uses (e.g. old curtains or swathes of fabric that can be wrapped for various costumes as opposed to a princess or nurse outfit that works for a single role); sensitively planting ideas to extend play; enriching children's experience through field trips and visitors to provide informed material for imaginative play scenarios; allowing long periods of time for play; encouraging children to plan their play explicitly; encouraging reflection after play (talking through what they played).

While the 'effective ingredients' of the 'Tools' curriculum that account for its positive effects on executive functions have not been conclusively identified, it seems likely that the emphasis on promoting mature imaginative play is important.

Mindfulness-based interventions

There is considerable interest in mindfulness-based interventions in education (Maynard, Solis, Miller, & Brendel, 2017). Some studies suggest the potential of such approaches for young children's executive functioning. Flook, Goldberg, Pinger, and Davidson (2015) implemented 20–30-minute sessions twice weekly based on attention and emotion regulation and found significant gains in cognitive flexibility, delay of gratification, sharing, teacher rated competence and end of term grades for learning and social-emotional development.

A much briefer intervention looked at the effects of four short sessions where children listened to sounds and were directed to attend to particular noises and locations (Murray, Theakston, & Wells, 2016). While most measures showed no difference between the intervention and control groups, the more surprising outcome, given the brevity of the intervention, was that the children who took part in attention training performed significantly better on a delay of gratification task. Mindfulness-based activities might be useful for some children in honing their executive functions.

We turn now to some research-informed strategies that can be used to promote executive functions across activities.

Explicitly teaching the language associated with executive functions and modelling its meaning

While the term *executive function* may just be becoming familiar to readers, the vocabulary associated with children employing these skills is very familiar, and includes: listen; remember; pay attention; think; wait; imagine; wait; talk through; explain; rule. Many young children require help to understand these terms. Executive functions can be promoted by introducing them explicitly, using visual symbols (e.g. represent 'pay attention' with an outline of a head and red lines from both the eyes and the brain leading to a person talking). Modelling of the requisite behaviour is also important (Truglio, Stefano, & Sanders, 2014).

Encouraging children to adopt a role

Many practitioners automatically use a technique of suggesting roles to children, for example asking them to tiptoe like a mouse when they want them to move particularly quietly. Recent experimental research now highlights the potential of role taking for improving executive function. White and Carlson (2016) carried out a study entitled 'What would Batman do?' They presented young children with a task where they have to sort cards according to shifting criteria (e.g. first colour, then shape.). In one condition, children chose a television or book character and were encouraged to perform the task as though they were that character ('What would Batman/Dora the Explorer/Bob the Builder/Rapunzel do?). Children taking such a role achieved the best performance on the task. Adopting a role as a competent, favoured character may enable children to achieve their best performance. This strategy has obvious links with the perceived value of pretend play for executive functions, discussed above.

Pausing before action/decision-making

Practitioners are often aware that some children would benefit from pausing before action. The challenge is often how to find a way of encouraging a child to pause. Van de Sande, Segers, & Verhoeven (2016) asked some young children who were using a computer program for early literacy skills to tell each answer to a soft toy before entering it on the computer. Children in this condition outperformed those who played the same games but omitted the step of explaining their decisions to a soft toy. The soft toy condition involved two features that are often advocated for developing executive functions – talking though a plan and a delay. Ling, Wong, and Diamond (2016) have investigated the importance of delay in detail and posit that its importance lies in giving time for a strong but incorrect impulse to fade, thus enabling children to make better decisions (show stronger executive functioning). The tactic of explaining to a soft toy is one way to introduce a delay. Practitioners need to become adept at generating creative ways of introducing delay for impulsive children.

Cooling responses

The broad strategy of helping children *cool* their responses has some overlap with strategies already discussed. Adopting a role and pausing can be ways of *cooling* children's impulsive responses. Other strategies involve helping them to recognise when they are becoming angry or upset and encouraging them to react to their early warning signs by allowing themselves a little *time out* in a comfortable area such as the book corner. Walter Mishel's work based on the marshmallow experiment also suggests ways for children to *cool* their impulses (Mischel, 2014). Looking away from the marshmallows or thinking of their visual features and imagining them as tiny beanbags for little toys helped children's performance on the task (whereas constantly looking at them or thinking of their taste and their melt-in-the-mouth qualities were, not surprisingly, detrimental to performance).

Conclusion: the importance of recognising, scaffolding and challenging executive functions

The curriculum framework proposed by Preedy in Chapter 2 incorporates the development of executive functions across the curriculum. Enabling children to develop executive functions depends highly upon practitioners able to recognise opportunities to develop these skills within activities. For this it is helpful to consider each of the three categories into which executive functions are usually divided: working memory; inhibition; and cognitive flexibility/attention shifting. Practitioners need to scaffold the executive functions within a task for individual children, as appropriate. Children who are struggling to fulfil the demands of a task need support to meet them and reduction of the executive function requirements to the point where they can achieve success. Continued honing of executive functions requires practitioner oversight and monitoring to provide individual children with attainable levels of challenge.

Closing the attainment gap and enabling all children to *start right* requires the provision of environments that meet children's physical and psychological needs, with skilful scaffolding and challenge of their executive functions within a wide range of developmentally appropriate activities. The authors of this book have led the way in enabling this to be a reality.

References

Andrews, J., Robinson, D. & Hutchinson, J. (2017). Closing the Gap? Trends in Educational Attainment and Disadvantage. Education Policy Unit https://epi.org.uk/report/closing-the-gap/ (accessed 17 August 2017).

Best, J. & Miller, P. (2010). A Developmental Perspective on Executive Function. *Child Development*, 81(6), 1641–1660.

Blair, C. B. & Raver, C. C. (2014.). Closing the Achievement Gap through Modification of Neurocognitive and Neuroendocrine Function: Results from a Cluster Randomized Controlled Trial of an Innovative Approach to the Education of Children in Kindergarten. *PLoS ONE*, 9(*11*), 1–13.

Bodrova, E. & Leong, D. J. (2007). *Tools of the Mind. The Vygotskian Approach to Early Childhood Education* (2nd edn). Upper Saddle River, NJ: Pearson Merrill/Prentice Hall.

Bodrova, E., Leong, D. J. & Akhutina, T.V. (2011). When Everything New is Well-Forgotten Old: Vygotsky/Luria Insights in the Development of Executive Functions. *New Directions for Child and Adolescent Development*, 133, 11–28.

Center on the Developing Child Harvard University (2011). Building the Brain's 'Air Traffic Control' System: How Early Experiences Shape the Development of Executive Function. http://developingchild.harvard.edu/resources/building-the-brains-air-traffic-control-system-how-early-experiences-shape-the-development-of-executive-function/ (accessed 17 August 2017).

Deci, E. L. & Ryan, R. M. (2000). The 'What' and 'Why' of Goal Pursuits: Human Needs and the Self-Determination of Behavior. *Psychological Inquiry*, 11(4), 227–268.

DfE (Department for Education) (2012). *Statutory Framework for the Early Years Foundation Stage 2012*. http://webarchive.nationalarchives.gov.uk/20130404110654/https://www.education.gov.uk/publications/standard/AllPublications/Page1/DFE-00023-2012 (accessed 17 August 2017).

DfE (Department for Education) (2014). *Statutory Framework for the Early Years Foundation Stage: Setting the Standards for Learning, Development and Care for Children from Birth to Five.* https://www.foundationyears.org.uk/eyfs-statutory-framework/ (accessed 17 August 2017).

DfES (Department for Education and Skills) (2007). *The Early Years Foundation Stage; Setting the Standards for Learning, Development and Care for Children from Birth to Five.* Nottingham; DfES Publications.

Diamond, A. (2010). The Evidence Base for Improving School Outcomes by Addressing the Whole Child and by Addressing Skills and Attitudes, Not Just Content. *Early Education and Development*, 21(5), 780–793.

Diamond, A. (2011). Biological and Social Influences on Cognitive Control Processes Dependent on Prefrontal Cortexes. *Progress in Brain Research*, 189, 319–339.

Diamond, A. (2012). Activities and Programs that Improve Children's Executive Functions. *Current Directions in Psychological Science*, 21(5), 335–341.

Diamond, A. (2015). Research that Moves us Closer to a World Where each Child Thrives. *Research in Human Development*, 12(3–4), 288–294.

Diamond, A., Barnett, W. S., Thomas, J. & Munro, S. (2007). The Early Years: Preschool Program Improves Cognitive Control. *Science*, 318(5855), 1387–1388.

Diamond, A. & Lee, K. (2011). Interventions Shown to Aid Executive Function Development in Children 4 to 12 Years Old. *Science*, 333, 959–964.

Diamond, A. & Ling, D. S. (2016). Conclusions about Interventions, Programs, and Approaches for Improving Executive Functions that Appear Justified and those that, despite Much Hype, Do Not. *Developmental Cognitive Neuroscience*, 18, 34–48.

Early Education supported by the Department of Education (2012). *Development Matters in the Early Years Foundation Stage*. London: Early Education

Education Endowment Fund https://educationendowmentfoundation.org.uk/

Flook, L., Goldberg, S. B., Pinger, L. & Davidson, R. J. (2015). Promoting Prosocial Behavior and Self-Regulatory Skills in Preschool Children through a Mindfulness-based Kindness Curriculum. *Developmental Psychology*, 51(1), 44–51.

Garon, N., Bryson, S. E. & Smith, I. M. (2008). Executive Function in Preschoolers: A Review Using an Integrative Framework. *Psychological Bulletin*, 134(1), 31–60.

Hackman, D. A. & Farah, M. J. (2009). Socioeconomic Status and the Developing Brain. *Trends in Cognitive Sciences*, 13(2), 65–73.

Ling, D. S., Wong, C. D. & Diamond, A. (2016). Do Children Need Reminders on the Day-Night Task, or Simply some Way to Prevent them from Responding too Quickly? *Cognitive Development*, 33(4), 395–401.

Maynard, B. R., Solis, M. R., Miller, V. L. & Brendel, K. E. (2017). Mindfulness-Based Interventions for Improving Academic Achievement, Behavior and Socio-Emotional Functioning of Primary and Secondary Students: A Systematic Review. https://www.campbellcollaboration.org/media/k2/attachments/Maynard_Mindfulness_Title.pdf (accessed 17 August 2017).

McClelland, M. M. & Wanless, S. B. (2012). Growing up with Assets and Risks: The Importance of Self-regulation for Academic Achievement. *Research in Human Development*, 9(4), 278–297.

Mischel, W. (2014). *The Marshmallow Test. Why Self-control is the Engine of Success*. New York, NY: Hachette Book Group.

Mischel, W., Shoda, Y. & Rodriguez, M. L. (1989). Delay of Gratification in Children. *Science*, 244, 933–938.

Miyake, A. & Friedman, N. P. (2012). The Nature and Organisation of Individual Differences in Executive Functions: Four General Conclusions. *Current Directions in Psychological Science*, 21(1), 8–14.

Moffitt, T. E., Arseneault, L., Belsky, D., Dickson, N., Hancox, R. J., Harrington, Houtsa, R., Poultonc, R., Roberts, B. W., Rossa, S., Searse, M. R., Murray Thomsong, W. & Caspi, A. (2011). A Gradient of Childhood Self-control Predicts Health, Wealth, and Public Safety. *Proceedings of the National Academy of Sciences of the United States of America*, 108(7), 2693–2698.

Morris, K. (2015). *Promoting Positive Behaviour in the Early Years*. Maidenhead: McGraw-Hill Open University Press.

Murray, J., Theakston, A. & Wells, A. (2016). Can the Attention Training Technique Turn One Marshmallow into Two? Improving Children's Ability to Delay Gratification. *Behaviour Research and Therapy*, 77, 34–39.

Raver, C. & Blair, C. (2016). Neuroscientific Insights: Attention, Working Memory, and Inhibitory Control. *Future of Children*, 26(2), 95–118.

Schmitt, S. A., McClelland, M. M., Tominey, S. L. & Acock, A. C. (2015). Strengthening School Readiness for Head Start Children: Evaluation of a Self-regulation Intervention. *Early Childhood Research Quarterly*, 30, 20–31.

Shaheen, S. (2013). Motor Assessment in Pediatric Neuropsychology: Relationships to Executive Function. *Applied Neuropsychology: Child*, 2 116–124.

Steenebergen-Hu, S., Olszewski-Kubilius, P. & Calvert, E. (2015). *Title Registration for a Systematic Review: School-Based Executive Functioning Interventions for Improving Executive Functions, Academic, Social-Emotional, and Behavioral Outcomes in School-Age Children and Adolescents: A Systematic Review and Meta-Analysis.* The Campbell Collaboration https://www.campbellcollaboration.org/library/school-based-executive-functioning-interventions-school-age-children.html (accessed 17 August 2017).

Tominey, S. L. & McClelland, M. M. (2011). Red Light, Purple Light: Findings From a Randomized Trial Using Circle Time Games to Improve Behavioral Self-Regulation in Preschool. *Early Education & Development*, 22(3), 489–519.

Truglio, R. T., Stefano, A. Z. & Sanders, J. S. (2014). Sesame Street Puts Self-Regulation Skills at the Core of School Readiness. *Zero to Three* (November), 24–32.

Van de Sande, E., Segers, E. & Verhoeven, L. (2016). Supporting Executive Functions during Children's Preliteracy Learning with the Computer. *Journal of Computer Assisted Learning*, 32(5), 468–480.

Vygotsky, L. (1978). *Mind in Society*. Cambridge, MA: MIT Press (original work published in 1930).

White, R. E. & Carlson, S. M. (2016). What would Batman Do? Self-distancing Improves Executive Function in Young Children. *Developmental Science*, 19(3), 419–426.

Zelazo, P. D. & Carlson, S. M. (2012). Hot and Cool Executive Function in Childhood and Adolescence: Development and Plasticity. *Child Development Perspectives*, 6(4), 354–360.

8

CREATING SUCCESSFUL LEARNING ENVIRONMENTS IN THE EARLY YEARS

A case study

Samantha Steed

Introduction

The overarching theme of early childhood constructivist pedagogies is that in order to support learning, practitioners need to look at how they are teaching from a *child's* perspective. According to Dewey (1859–1952), Vygotsky (1896–1934) and Piaget (1896–1980) learning is an active, not a passive, process where knowledge is constructed not acquired. That learning is best achieved when children communicate with each other, constructing their understanding in meaningful contexts through self-discovery.

Dewey (1938) strongly rejected the view that educators should engage their pupils in rote style learning. Instead he provided practical workshops for children where they were able to think for themselves and use previously acquired knowledge to construct and evaluate their ideas. In a Vygotskian classroom, there is an emphasis on assisted discovery and questioning. This social interaction is thought to promote comprehension of concepts that children may not gain on their own. Pupils in a Piaget-inspired classroom are also free to make discoveries at their own pace in an environment that caters sensitively to a child's readiness for learning and where uniqueness is accepted.

Dr Amanda Gummer (2015), a widely recognised play expert, suggests that parents are often surprised at what their children learn when given the freedom to play, without the usual constraints of planned outcomes and adult directed teaching – this was certainly the case with the *Play Partners Project* detailed in Chapter 6 of this book. Gummer suggests that learning through play is beneficial to children as they learn invaluable skills about themselves and their environment, which most likely cannot be taught in a traditional classroom. She argues that the provision of a collaborative learning environment that emphasises authentic tasks is fundamental to a child's early learning.

Walsh and Gardner (2005), when assessing the quality of early years environments, asked questions such as: How experimental is the setting and, to what extent do children experience flow, immersion, sense of control and unconscious concentration? Based on their research they recommend that quality learning environments provide opportunities for children's natural curiosity to manifest itself promoting motivation, concentration, independence, confidence, well-being, social interaction, respect, and higher order thinking skills.

The Steiner Waldorf Schools arose out of a philosophy that promotes universal human values within a creative learning environment that enables children to enjoy unhurried learning without *hot-housing*. This chapter explores whether it is possible to provide children with an environment that gives them the opportunities to communicate, play and think for themselves whilst at the same time ensuring that they achieve the highest standards academically and personally.

Creating effective learning environments

The first priority is to create an environment that is physically and emotionally secure and safe. Part of feeling secure is being able to attach to familiar people in familiar places with a space that belongs to you. Once we have ensured children's welfare, health and safety we can turn to creating the optimal learning environment.

The Reggio Emilia approach (Gandini, 2008) specifically links learning to the environment. The environment is often referred to as the third teacher providing a variety of spaces for children to experience and explore. The environment is carefully studied, from the physical structure to the internal layout of the various centres or exploration places. According to Ceppi and Zini (1998), who were primary researchers involved in a meta-project in Reggio Emilia, a place for educating children must include the following important aspects: relationships between subjects, actions, experiences and language, transparencies, light, virtual spaces, sounds and the importance of materials.

Duncan et al. (2007) suggest that nature is the natural teacher for all human kind. That as children's connection to nature is primary, timeless and, core to their being, an effective learning environment must include the outdoors.

Jarman (2007) has highlighted the impact that indoor and outdoor spaces, resources and colour can have on children's emotional security, well-being and learning. She suggests that it is critical to understand how the physical space should connect with its intention and that it is essential to tune into the environment from the learner's perspective. To do this, it is vital to observe, reflect and then make informed decisions about the way that children interact with the environment.

In an attempt to provide the best, practitioners may be tempted to overcrowd the learning environment with furniture, toys and equipment. This leads to over-stimulation of children across all of the senses, making it difficult to process information and to think. The management of noise levels and the reduction of background noise are essential so that children can hear and process language. Carpeting, curtains and drapes can help to dampen undesirable noise as well as being part of an attractive environment. Hanging wind chimes or planting long grasses helps to create calming sounds. The soothing colours of nature – greens, blues, browns and creams are often more conducive to learning.

Large open plan spaces can be daunting for young children and offer little in the way of security for a young child leaving his or her carer for the first time. Many young children benefit from secluded corners and irregular shaped enclosures. Jarman (2007) advocates the creation of smaller contained spaces, which she calls *Communication Friendly Spaces* within a larger environment; using fabrics and cushions to create softness in the space. Prescott (2008, p. 34) also argues that *hard* materials give the message *you had better shape up and do what the environment requires – it's not going to give in to you.*

Provocations are designed to provoke thinking experiences in response to children's interests and ideas enabling them to practise, test, construct and deconstruct their ideas and theories. According to Prescott (1994) provocations can be simple, complex or super complex. Simple provocations are those with essentially one function; complex those with two; and super complex those with more than two. For example, water in a tray is a simple unit. If the practitioner adds some dinosaurs it becomes a complex unit. Adding some rocks and plants creates a super-complex unit. The more complex the materials, the more play and learning they provide. When a practitioner sets up a provocation, she should listen and engage in the child's thinking.

Provocations that promote pretend play require the ability to transform objects and actions symbolically; for example, by pretending to be a fireman or mummy. In dramatic play children develop their receptive and expressive language skills (listening and speaking), they expand their capacity for imagining, they imitate life around them, build their attention and engagement capacity, learn how to negotiate with other children and their thoughts, ideas and strategies, put mathematical understandings to use in meaningful/playful context (counting sorting etc.), practise problem-solving skills with their peers and build their working vocabulary. The use of real objects such as placemats, cups, forks, wooden plates, tins, wooden spoons etc. can be more engaging and meaningful to role play when chosen carefully.

From theory into practice: a case study

As Principal of Ranches Primary School in Dubai I have been working with the staff to create a secure and safe environment that enables children to play, actively exploring and learning across the curriculum. Creating an inclusive and open ethos where families can contribute to their children's well-being and learning is important to us. An example of this approach is when we invited parents to bring in family portraits in a picture frame of their choosing. Many children were reassured by the presence of their family portrait during their settling-in journey. Similarly, children who felt secure in their surroundings continued to be motivated to look at the photographs, taking comfort and visible pride in the familiarity of their family members. The shared interactions observed between the children and their families

FIGURE 8.1 An example of a Family Photograph Tree. Children enjoy talking about their families. The photographs provide a link between home and school, helping children to develop confidence and self-awareness

when taking time to pause and reflect on the photographs have been invaluable. One parent described this as a *feel good* display.

We have carefully reviewed our use of space, resources and storage. Natural resources have been used to back our display boards; pebbles and shells support the children's self-registration process. Using a variety of boxes, baskets etc. that only hold a few dinosaurs, or a small selection of construction equipment, enables children to engage more easily with the resources.

Building up a collection of natural resources began with items found in the immediate environment (leaves, shells, bark and twigs, rocks and pebbles). These provide the children with many opportunities to develop their understanding of concepts such as *big and little, same and different, long and short, few and many, heavy and light*.

In the following passage, a teacher explains how she has organised her classroom.

> *In my classroom, I have tried to create calm and welcoming spaces. I plan how resources are arranged carefully, setting up invitations to play that are open ended. Provocations are created that I think will either spark a child's interest or enhance a current interest. I am always searching for interesting items that I can use in my classroom; an Arabic jug, blue stones, miniature logs, a large shell, because I want to encourage my class to be curious. In the UAE, we have to work hard to ensure children are exposed to different kinds of nature because it is not as easily accessible as it is in the UK. That is why you will find plants, mirrors, wooden furniture and many more natural items in my classroom.*

FIGURE 8.2 An example of a Family Message Tree where parents write messages of hope about their child, e.g. I hope that my child will make friends and be happy

FIGURE 8.3 It is important that practitioners make resources available in a way that allows children to make choices

FIGURE 8.4 An example of a 'provocation' using natural resources

Placing invitation tables outside of the classroom is an enticement for children to enter the classroom. A collection of interesting and intentionally organised materials in a location visible from the classroom door sparks a child's curiosity.

We use a range of provocations to enhance children's language and thought. The provocations in Figure 8.7 show the use of real objects including builders' bricks, deckchairs, baskets and tyres.

FIGURE 8.5   An example of an Invitation Table

FIGURE 8.6   An example of using natural items for play-based activities

A practitioner explains how she set up a simple provocation activity consisting of a bowl of soapy water:

> *The children came up with the idea of a car wash after I'd put out some bubbles and water for them to splash with when it was hot. The children were observed putting their scooter wheels into the water tray 'for cleaning'. So, I added a few sponges, a till and some*

FIGURE 8.7, 8.8, 8.9   Some examples of a 'Complex Provocation' using some real–world materials

> *writing materials. The children then spent about 20 minutes in dramatic play, interacting with each other and developing new vocabulary. Some children demonstrated how to take turns and some discussed the concept of paying with money and writing receipts. Very little adult guidance was needed during their play, however, in subsequent sessions an adult gently prompted the children to explore questions related to capacity and materials.*

The following account is from a Reception class teacher explaining how she used herbs as a provocation following the children's interest in the senses:

> *The natural materials and unusual smells instantly captured their interest. I had initially thought the provocation would provide an engaging opportunity to develop fine motor skills, with pupils cutting, grinding and pinching the herbs. As is so often the case, the children took the activity in their own imaginative direction. In addition to developing motor skills they were observed eagerly sharing vocabulary to describe the different textures and smells of the herbs. Ensuing activities were later set up to further develop these skills, including 'smelly bottles', sorting materials and writing about different textures.*

In-the-moment planning

It is vital that practitioners have the necessary skills to identify the children's interests and know when and how to intervene. *In-the-moment planning* is about capturing the children's current interests at a given time (Ephgrave, 2018).

FIGURE 8.10 Using natural items to create a provocation

As described above, practitioners who have the freedom to follow the children's interests often have higher rates of engagement from the children. Laevers (2000) suggests that we bring adventure and serendipity into our settings. He advocates giving the practitioners confidence to let go of rigid planning and to support taking the perspective of the child seizing the golden opportunities that are there. Adults can also incorporate elements of particular objectives that they would like the children to learn creating a balance of child and adult led activities. Katz (1995) agrees that educative experiences that evolve increase engagement and problem-solving skills more so than *frivolous one-shot activities.*

Reflections

The child's environment contributes greatly to how he or she feels, acts and behaves. Prominent early years philosophers have asserted that children learn the most when they are able to be active agents in their environment. Katz (1995, p. 120) uses the phrase 'a bottom-up perspective of quality'; that is, the way in which a setting is experienced by the participating children. These ideas are taken up by Walsh and Gardner (2005) who argue that the quality of an early years setting is principally determined by the way in which the learning and developmental needs of the main stakeholders – that is, the children – are met. The creation of an environment that is safe and secure, where children can work out how to interact with others and where exploration and freedom are valued, is essential for giving children the right start to their education. Nurtured, healthy, happy children are able to achieve highly, both academically and personally.

References

Ceppi, G. & Zini, M. (1998). *Children, Spaces, Relations: Metaproject for an Environment for Young Children*. Reggio Emilia, Italy: Reggio Children.

Dewey, J. (1938). *Experience and Education*. New York: Macmillan.

Duncan, J., Dowsett, C., Claessens, A., Magnuson, K., Huston, A., Klebanov, P., Pagani, L., Feinstein, L., Engel, M., Brooks-Gunn, J., Duckworth, H. & Japel, C. (2007). School readiness and later achievement. *Developmental Psychology*, 43, 1428–1446.

Ephgrave, E. (2018). Planning in the Moment with Young Children: A Practical Guide for Early Years Practitioners and Parents. Oxon: Routledge

Gandini, L. (2008). Introduction to the fundamental values of the education of young children in Reggio Emilia (adapted from Gandini, L. (2008). *Introduction to the schools of Reggio Emilia*). In L. Gandini, S. Etheredge, S. & L. Hill (Eds), *Insights and Inspirations: Stories of Teachers and Children from North America* (pp. 24–27). Worchester, MA: Davis Publications.

Gummer, A. (2015). *Play: Fun Ways to Help Your Child Develop in the First Five Years*. London: Vermilion.

Jarman, E. (2007). *Communication Friendly Spaces: Improving Speaking and Listening Skills in The Early Years Foundation Stage*. Basic Skills Agency.

Katz, L. G. (1995). *Talks with Teachers of Young Children: A Collection*. Norwood, NJ: Ablex.

Laevers, F. (2000). Forward to basics! Deep level learning and the experiential approach. *Early Years*, 20(2), 20–29.

Prescott, E. (1994). The physical environment. *Exchange Magazine* March/April: Issue 100.

Prescott, E. (2008). The physical environment: A powerful regulator of experience. Child Care Information Exchange, April/May, 2008, 34–37.

Walsh, G. & Gardner, J. (2005). Assessing the quality of early years learning environments. *Early Childhood Research and Practice*, 7(1), 27–57.

9

CREATIVITY IN THE EARLY YEARS

Ruth Churchill Dower

What is creativity?

Scholars around the world have defined creativity as being inventive, original or innovative; turning a new idea into something that hasn't been made before, creating a new product, or an idea that is both novel and useful in a particular social context (Schore & Marks-Tarlow, 2017). I don't disagree but, from the many hundreds of creative encounters I have experienced with young children, I think it's something even more fundamental than this. It's about being able to discover and express your emotions, your passions, your ideas, your resourcefulness and your unique view on life in a variety of ways that are unlimited by normal constraints such as time, money, academic standards, stress or peer pressure.

The National Advisory Committee on Creative and Cultural Education (NAC-CCE) defines creativity as: 'Imaginative activity fashioned so as to produce outcomes that are both original and of value' (NACCCE, 1999, p. 30). Since then, eminent psychologists and neuroscientists have proposed a definition closer to our experience, which is based on the knowledge that the brain creates strategies to cope with, assimilate and process novel situations. They propose that a child's creativity is intrinsically linked to his early experiences of affection, attachment, self-regulation and love. Essentially, the positive emotions and behaviours that arouse the curiosity, inspiration, novelty, joy and play in babies to be creative are largely triggered by loving interactions, which makes the argument for love and attachment to be a central tenet of early education as discussed in previous chapters of this book.

The problem is that, when it comes to observing and 'measuring' children's creativity for the sake of identifying and supporting their learning progress, early years professionals working with young children, including teachers, head teachers, teaching assistants, practitioners, childminders, nannies, setting managers, learning

support assistants, playgroup staff and play workers often don't feel creative themselves or know what their own creative faculties are. Therefore, how can they feel
competent in mapping out this area successfully with their children?

This is not the same with most core areas of learning and development in the
Early Years Foundation Stage (EYFS) where practitioners will have had at least
some basic training or experience, if not during their pre-service or professional
training, then during their own time at school. We would be outraged if early
years teachers were not adequately trained to teach literacy and numeracy, but, it
seems, the same urgency is not assigned to teaching creativity with many teacher
training courses restricting this area to supporting children's basic arts skills, which
are not the same as their creative thinking or doing skills. Many parents also seem
unaware of what creativity means and how it could be of importance in the home.
Yet experts in many fields including education, science, health, business and the
public sector are telling us with increasing urgency how important creativity is for
our children.

There is a strong body of evidence pointing to the importance and value of early
childhood arts and creative practice, for children's learning and development, for
family and community, and for society in general. The following literature review
highlights that quality creative experiences in early childhood can have a significant impact on children's learning and development, with, in many cases, life-long
impact.

FIGURE 9.1 Why is creativity so important in young children's lives?

Source: © Rachel Brooke.

Siraj-Blatchford et al. (2002) and Jayatilaka (2010) link creative or cultural experiences that make an impact in early childhood and involve children experimenting with new ideas, techniques and materials to subsequent abilities in the arts that will be useful throughout life. There is also evidence (Sousa, 2006) that training in specific art forms can impact the brain's development in other areas of cognition. For example, music activates the same areas of the brain that are activated during reading (in tasks relating to decoding, tone and phonological awareness) and in mathematical processing, especially in tasks common to both such as counting, ratios or intervals, creating patterns and sequences, tone groupings and spatial reasoning skills. Creative approaches can lead to a direct improvement in academic achievements in numeracy and literacy (Duffy, 2010) and help children make sense of a range of knowledge and skills, e.g. language development (Heath & Wolf, 2005), numeracy (Sousa, 2006), reading and literacy (Catterall, 1997; CLA, 2012), personal, social and emotional development (Duffy, 2006), physical development (O'Connor & Daly, 2016), developing sensory and motor skills (Grace, 2018), spiritual development and understanding of people and cultures (Bamford, 2006; Duffy, 2010).

Creativity promotes strong physical growth e.g. through dance and movements such as pushing, pulling, crawling, standing, running, spinning, climbing, etc. as well as sensory health and vitality. As discussed in Chapters 3 and 4 of this book, movement-based activities help children to use their bodies as vehicles for sensory expression by developing a properly functioning nervous system. Mark making, drawing, crafting and singing help with the coordination and muscle memory required for motor development as well as supporting the healthy development of the vestibular (motion and balance) and proprioception (body position awareness) systems required for sensory learning (Grace, 2018; O'Connor & Daly, 2016). The strength and quality of a child's physical development, or lack of, has a direct impact on their emotional wellbeing and learning potential (Goddard Blythe, 2004; Grace, 2018).

Early childhood arts and cultural activities can significantly strengthen parent–child bonds and engage families in their children's learning, providing a positive focus for shared experience and communication (Ipsos Mori, 2009, Jayatilaka, 2010; Schore & Marks-Tarlow, 2017). Creative, play-based experiences in early childhood can help children communicate authentically and effectively, expressing their feelings, emotions, thoughts and ideas in non-verbal and pre-verbal ways (Duffy, 2010). It can help them develop curiosity and critical awareness, and improve their ability to make choices and apply scientific reasoning, leading to a better understanding of themselves and others, and helping to build respectful and positive relationships (Bruce, 2005). Early childhood arts can help develop intrinsic human qualities, such as love, self-expression, independence, self-awareness and empathy, self-esteem, resilience and imagination (Bamford, 2006; Cizek, 1921; NACCCE, 1999; Schore & Marks-Tarlow, 2017; Witkin, 1974). As well as helping to preserve our cultural heritage, creativity enables young children to develop their own languages that help shape their sense of identity and individuality as well as their identity as part of a larger – local and global – community (Bamford, 2006; Duffy, 2010). Creativity strengthens human connection by building trust and connecting children across cultural, religious, generational and socio-economic divides. It breaks down language barriers (NCB, 2010) and cultural prejudices or societal differences, and leads to decreased social problems (Barnett & Ackermann, 2006), reduced inequality and increased creativity (Perkins & Orly, 1999).

Creativity promotes positive mental and behavioural health. Numerous studies demonstrate how creative activities that are linked to our emotions can help to make positive neural connections, reduce anxiety, build self-esteem and self-confidence, increase a sense of agency and empowerment, develop strong self-regulatory processes, increase the immune function and decrease a reliance on health care (Brown & Sax, 2013; Catterall, 1997; CLA, 2012; Duffy, 2006; Elias & Berk, 2002; Mualem & Klein, 2013; Muñiz, Silver & Stein, 2014; NACCCE, 1999; Pennebaker, 2004; Perkins & Orly, 1999; Schore & Marks-Tarlow, 2017; Witkin, 1974; White, Lord & Sharp, 2015).

When introduced into early childhood training and professional development, creative approaches can help to improve the practice and pedagogy in early childhood settings, including professionals' confidence and understanding of child development (Perkins & Orly, 1999; Rinaldi, 2001).

Stimulating and compelling experiences at museums, galleries, theatres, libraries, or dance, arts or music venues will offer many parents the ideas, confidence and resources to play with their children as a natural part of everyday life (Oskala et al., 2009). Collaborations that bring together different perspectives from arts or cultural professionals, early years professionals, children and parents can result in a much deeper understanding of, and attention to, a child's needs and interests (Churchill Dower, Hogan, Hoy & Sims, 2006; Clark, Griffiths & Taylor, 2003). It can also stimulate a much deeper level of ideas and solutions-generation when creating with co-learners. This leads to a more sustainable learning progression, raising the quality of learning, and a sense of fulfilment for educators and children both immediately and later on in life (NACCCE, 1999; Duffy, 2010).

Early years creative experiences are fun and elicit joy. It's a space to forget our worries and find ourselves immersed in the present moment. In this place, the mind is most open to spontaneity and inspiration, leading to the joy of simply being, enjoying and, sometimes, expressing ourselves (Schore & Marks-Tarlow, 2017; Witkin, 1974).

How important is creativity in society?

A global benchmark study by Adobe (2012) on the state of creativity in five world countries shows that eight in ten people feel that unlocking their creativity is critical to economic growth and nearly two-thirds of respondents feel creativity is valuable to society, yet a striking minority – only one in four people – believe they are living up to their own creative potential. More than half of those surveyed feel that creativity is being stifled by their education systems, and many believe creativity is taken for granted (52 per cent globally, 70 per cent in the United States). Sir Ken Robinson (2007) powerfully highlights this issue:

> One of the problems is that too often our educational systems don't enable students to develop their natural creative powers. Instead, they promote uniformity and standardisation. The result is that we're draining people of their creative possibilities and producing a workforce that's conditioned to prioritise conformity over creativity.

The Future of Play study from the Lego Foundation (Ackermann et al., 2010) is a further illustration of the importance of spontaneity in order to stimulate creativity and play, and to build deep relationships between children and adults through sharing a highly creative experience together. Yet many educators and parents feel strongly that the education and economic systems they live and work in are increasingly stifling the opportunities for spontaneous learning and play. Early years educators report that they have to spend more and more time on assessing and averting possible risk, and on observing and assessing children's progress rather than playing with them and using their professional judgement to support progress (Bradbury & Roberts-Holmes, 2016).

While necessary to help us spot the gaps in learning, assessments appear to be becoming increasingly reductive, with a disproportionate focus on literacy and numeracy at a younger and younger age, despite the plethora of expert knowledge about how young children develop at different ages and stages during this period (Hood, 2017; Duffy, 2006). As described in Chapters 2, 5 and 6 of this book, long-running recession coupled with ill-fitting government policies on childcare contribute to parents working longer hours and having less time with their children.

Social commentator, Daniel Pink, stresses how the key senses developed in the brain such as playfulness, empathy, creativity and a sense of meaning are essential for children to thrive in the future:

> The keys to the kingdom are changing. The future belongs to a very different kind of person with a different kind of mind: creators and empathizers, pattern recognisers and meaning makers. These people – artists, inventors, designers, story tellers, caregivers, consolers, big picture thinkers – will now reap society's richest rewards and share its greatest joys.
>
> *(Pink, 2006, p. 1)*

Although everyone is born with an innate potential to be creative, the evidence reviewed in this chapter indicates that creativity for many children is a small part of their lives and can be virtually lost. Adults who do not follow an artistic pathway tend to move away from a close sense of their own creativity usually after late childhood/teenage years. This is at a time when their critical awareness matures and judgement-based perceptions are built on what constitutes 'good' art, or what a drawing/piece of artwork 'should' look like.

How is creativity different from the arts?

We naturally associate creativity with having arts skills or producing art products. Franz Cizek (1865–1946), an Austrian genre and portrait painter best known as a teacher and reformer of art education, and for starting the Child Art Movement in Vienna in 1897, believed that every child had a natural tendency towards creative and artistic expression, which should be fostered through imaginative leaning environments. According to Cizek (1921), 'Art is a natural aspect of human development from birth, the absence of which impairs mental growth and social fitness' (Bamford, 2006, p. 32).

This idea has been supported by other early childhood theorists, including Dewey (an American philosopher, psychologist and educational reformer whose ideas have been influential in education and social reform through his books, *Democracy and Education* (1916), *Art as Experience* (1934) and *Experience and Education* (1938)), Lowenfield (a professor of art education at the Pennsylvania State University, best known for *Creative and Mental Growth* (1947) – the single most influential textbook in art education, and for his theory of stages in artistic development), Bruner (one of the best known and influential psychologists of the twentieth century whose book, *The Culture of Education* (1996) influenced the acknowledgement of culture in education) and Rogoff (an educator and psychologist whose interests lie in understanding and communicating the different learning thrusts between cultures, expressed in her book, *The Cultural Nature of Human Development* (2003).

The arts are an important vehicle for creativity, but creativity does not reside exclusively in the domain of the arts. People can enjoy and express their creativity in a number of ways throughout everyday life, whether it's whilst cooking, gardening, going for a walk or tidying up. If these activities involve expressing passion, resourcefulness, joyfulness, playfulness, spontaneity, transformation, critical evaluation, new ideas and new solutions, then they are involving creativity to differing degrees, even if people don't recognise that this is what is happening.

How do we support young children in discovering and nurturing their creativity?

The above experts along with centuries of creative thinkers and doers have demonstrated how being creative happens in stages as ideas are spontaneously or deliberately generated, evaluated, extended, reflected upon and refined. Some people spend a lot of time at one end of this process, others at the other end. To learn how to extend your creativity requires a sense of knowing where you are on this scale and how to move forward without destroying the core spontaneity that generates further creativity.

Creativity is more than just developing new skills and ideas. Something deep inside our core changes when we are creative, something that speaks to both our identity and spirit. As Sir Ken Robinson states: 'Only through the arts and by being creative can children explore the inner world of their imagination and feeling ... the world that is uniquely them' (Robinson, 2012).

FIGURE 9.2 Creativity comes in all shapes and sizes

Source: © Ruth Churchill Dower.

This is the place inside ourselves where we develop our meaning, make sense of who we are and what our purpose is. It's where we have our most profound thoughts and questions about life, and from where our motivation and inspiration grow. I believe that creativity is programmed into our blueprint and, unless we recognise this and enable children's inherent creativity to be nurtured and matured, they may never know what it is to experience this powerful sense of possibility and purpose, of self-control and mastery within themselves.

Creativity may also be sparked through the influence of others including parents, teachers, significant adults and other children. They can help children to imagine themselves in situations they have not yet experienced but that can add meaning to their lives. Their actions and words can help the enjoyment of an experience adding value and meaning beyond anything experienced before. Frequently collaborating with others, experiencing their ideas and filters on life, takes our creativity to a new level that might not have been possible on our own.

Vygotsky's (1978) description of the *zone of proximal development* (ZPD) is helpful when considering how to support young children's creativity. Vygotsky describes the ZPD as the space where a child can achieve more with someone's help than he could have achieved without that help. It is the space where the child can be challenged and inspired to develop his thinking and actions without being too frustrated (because it's too hard), and without being too bored (because it's too easy). It's the space where the child can move beyond what he thought he was capable of to be even more creative.

Vygotsky intended this theory to reduce the teacher-led instruction common in the 1930s and to argue against the use of academic, knowledge-based tests as a means to gauge students' intelligence, but it remained unfinished due to his untimely death in 1936 at the age of 38. The concept of being supported and challenged to fully develop a child's learning potential was built on further by early childhood psychologist, Bruner (1915–2016) through his concept of 'scaffolding'. This is where young children's thinking and ideas are supported to focus on key information or knowledge through developmentally appropriate questioning as they play. As the child forms the knowledge and understanding, the amount of 'scaffolding' required is gradually reduced, just as with scaffolding around a house, until the skills or understanding of a particular concept are complete (Wood, Bruner & Ross, 1976, p. 90).

Being creative in collaboration with others is just like this – we are experiencing their carefully crafted propositions and using them to extend our own creative thinking, ideas and solutions, thereby enabling our creative competence to be extended beyond what we were capable of achieving on our own. This is how we build our resilience, confidence, capability, independence, spontaneity, imagination, self-regulation, critical awareness and scientific reasoning. Isn't this just what we should be doing with our youngest children every day?

For these reasons, I suggest that early education and care needs to nurture highly creative teaching and learning environments as described in the previous chapter. Not only will such environments help strengthen synaptic connections and make them more useful and usable later on in life, they will also enable children to express their ideas and needs more fluently in a range of languages whilst they are still very young. Such expression is vital to enable each child's needs to be met, their ideas validated and developed, and for them to become more fulfilled, better understood and less frustrated.

> By encouraging creativity and imagination, we are promoting children's ability to explore and comprehend their world and increasing their opportunities to make new connections and reach new understandings.
>
> *(Duffy, 2006, p. 9)*

FIGURE 9.3 Imagination enables children to explore their world

Source: © Rachel Brooke.

How can educators and parents support children's creativity?

As well as having their creativity ignited, children need opportunities to practise their creative aptitudes and skills within a supportive environment that validates their attempts to learn and grow (Duffy, 2010, pp. 20–21; Ellyatt, 2010, p. 90). In this environment children can achieve a level of mastery in creating and expressing their interests and ideas, which has a positive impact on their learning across all areas.

To create this environment, adults should be confident to express their own creativity and model the trying out of different techniques for their children, as well as scaffolding and encouraging children's own ideas. While, initially, educators and parents may be concerned with the quality of a creation and feel they are not suitably qualified to produce a piece of artwork that stands up to inspection by another adult, immersing yourselves in the process of creativity helps enormously to shift that focus away from worrying about the outcome and enables you to focus on the enjoyment of creating. Creativity should definitely include an element of fun! It can be hard work sometimes in exploring different possible solutions to a problem or trying to help children think about an issue or work as a team, but the process of learning, working and expressing creatively should also be enjoyable and interesting to the creator, whether that is you as an adult or the child.

Whether introducing stories, collage, clay, photography, music, weaving, wood-working, singing or dancing, adults need not worry about what they or their creation looks like, as your children are unlikely to be bothered by this. If some music makes you want to move, then let your body move. If a particular combination of colours and textures makes you want to paint a particular shape or pattern, then paint it. Have a go and get involved! The quicker we can move our own inhibitions out of the way, the more expressive and confident our children will become in their own creative processes.

> Free-flowing processes can be inhibited in many ways, one of which comes from giving people a fear of failure. . . . In order to learn we need to be in a position in which we are open to receiving ideas, processes, sensations and feelings – the gamut of human experience; we need to have been allowed to respond to these experiences in ways that aren't inhibited through being told that this or that response is wrong or insufficient.
>
> *(Rosen, 2010, p. 10)*

Research by psychologists Carl Rogers, Abraham Maslow and others confirms that when we are deeply immersed in creative processes, the sense of being self-conscious is replaced by a sense of enjoyment and community. Professor Mihalyi Csikszentmihalyi described this as the state of 'flow', when someone is focussed so intently on the process or activity being undertaken that they lose themselves to the enjoyment and satisfaction of it and the experience of learning becomes its own reward (Csikszentmihalyi, 1996, p. 110). This state is very similar to the one we experience when we see our children deeply immersed in their play, so we know what it looks like even if we haven't felt it for ourselves. It is a state where goals, objectives and external rewards fly out of the window as the excitement of the present moment becomes all that matters.

A state of flow is very important to foster with young children as it allows then to reach a much deeper level of thinking and learning than normal. Children question possibilities or explore relationships between ideas and things over time. When we relentlessly follow a timetable asking children to tidy up what they are playing with before snack, lunch, afternoon snack, outdoor play, story time and home time, we are effectively limiting the flow and depth of their thinking to a superficial level that does not allow for deeper connections to be made. Much better to observe those children whose play scenarios should be preserved and allow them to return to the exploration of their ideas after the break (or sometimes bring the snack to them to limit the disruption of flow, if possible).

How do different art forms enable young children's learning?

Most art forms will foster a creative response in young children. They do this by stimulating the imagination, arousing curiosity, enabling exploration of different propositions, engaging with the senses, and allowing the child to create new meanings and make sense of the experiences they are having. Children create, store and recall their knowledge as memories that are articulated sometimes immediately; sometimes many days or weeks after they have been created; sometimes never. Whether articulated or not, all of their creative experiences will help to form a contextual tapestry through which existing knowledge is joined to new knowledge as children make sense of the things around them (Bruce, 2005; Duffy, 2006). This is one of the most important aspects of using different art forms to facilitate deeper levels of learning and creativity.

As they engage in creative experiences, children will communicate their feelings, emotions, ideas, questions and perspectives on the world around them including other children and adults they interact with. They may not yet have the capability to express these things in a verbal language, so the arts provide wonderful resources to help children represent what they mean using movement, colour, texture, gesture, sound and images. Different art forms can play different roles in helping babies and young children to explore, discover and communicate their meaning-making, as well as nurturing their imagination and creative potential. As adults, our job is to explore which creative approaches will work best to support our children's journeys of discovery.

Drama and role play can stimulate the same synapses that focus on spoken language; painting can stimulate the visual processing system that recalls memory or creates fantasy; movement, drawing and modelling link to the development of gross and fine motor skills (Sousa, 2006). From the UK cohort study Child of the New Century surveys, which happened at ages 3 and 5, mothers were asked how often they helped their child with reading and writing, and activities such as drawing and painting. The surveys found that children who had these types of interactions in their pre-school years displayed better behaviour and moods, and higher ability in reading and Maths (Child of the New Century, 2016). Dance has been found to increase the number of capillaries in the brain, which facilitates blood flow and therefore oxygen to the brain, thereby impacting on cognitive performance at the same time as supporting a child's healthy, physical development (O'Connor & Daly, 2016; Sousa, 2006). There is also a large body of evidence demonstrating how music-making in early childhood can develop the perception of different phonemes and the auditory cortex and hence aid the development of language learning as well as musical behaviour (Lonie, 2010, p. 13). As a result of this, several music education methods, including Suzuki, Kodaly, Orff and Dalcroze are designed to support children with developmentally appropriate musical activities from very young ages. The In Harmony programme (based on Venezuela's *El Systema* programme) is a good example of how a large scale approach to music-making in the foundation years can lead to enhanced academic achievement and engagement in learning, especially for children with special educational needs or those for whom music opportunities would not otherwise have been available (White et al., 2015).

If children are denied these experiences, for whatever reason (entitlement, economics, cultural, societal), the synapses that are predisposed to imagination, auditory, linguistic, physical or creative thinking skills may be pruned, making it difficult to reconnect those synapses further down the line, although not impossible. Which is why it is so important to make these opportunities available to young children as much as possible between birth and their school years.

Virtually all art forms are reported to lead to increased social and emotional development to varying degrees. One nationally representative study in the United States used data from the Early Childhood Longitudinal Study, Birth Cohort pre-school wave, which is a nationally representative dataset of children born in 2001. This study showed that children whose parents interacted creatively with them – such as singing to or with them or playing with construction toys and building blocks to create sculptures – at least three times per week had a higher likelihood of developing strong and sophisticated social skills, such as pro-social behaviours, compared with parents who reported interacting creatively with their child fewer than three times per week (Muñiz et al., 2014).

Several studies have emerged that focus on the relationship between arts partici-pation and emotion regulation, where the ability to control emotional affect and expression has improved significantly, along with children's ability to function, dur-ing and after arts interventions (Brown & Sax, 2013; Elias & Berk, 2002; Mualem & Klein, 2013, amongst others). Many of these studies also show direct relationship between the arts intervention and children's ability to achieve higher levels of self-motivation and self-esteem, both of which are essential skills for life.

Conclusion

Although creativity is one of the characteristics of effective learning identified in the EYFS the word *creative* is only mentioned four times in the entire EYFS guid-ance material, *Development Matters* (2012) (two referring to the creative process and two referring to creative thinking and problem solving), and is not mentioned at all in the entire EYFS curriculum. Guidance offered for measuring progress in the area of Expressive Arts and Design is specific to the skills and knowledge children might acquire in this area rather than how to nurture and apply their broader crea-tive faculties across all areas of learning.

Creativity is naturally associated with art skills and producing art products. How-ever, creativity is possible and should be included across the curriculum as it is an important part of early childhood development. The revised Early Years curriculum framework devised by Preedy in Chapter 2 of this book addresses this enormous gap. Creativity is part of young children *starting right* and is of increasing importance in the world of work, both now and in the future.

References

Ackermann, E., Gauntlett, D., Whitebread, D., Weckstrom, C., & Wolbers, T. (2010). *The future of play. Defining the role and value of play in the 21st century*. Billund, Denmark: The Lego Foundation.

Adobe (2012). *State of Create Global Benchmark Study*: www.adobe.com/aboutadobe/press-room/pressreleases/201204/042312AdobeGlobalCreativityStudy.html (accessed 31 August 2017).

Bamford, A. (2006). The Wow Factor: Global research compendium on the impact of the arts in education. Munster: Waxmann Verlag, pp.19–33.

Barnett, S. & Ackerman, D. (2006). Costs, benefits and long-term effects of early care and education programs: Recommendations and cautions for community developers. *Community Development: Journal of the Community Development Society*, 37(2), 86–100.

Bradbury, A. & Roberts-Holmes, G. (2016). *They are children . . . not robots, not machines. The introduction of Reception Baseline Assessment.* The Association of Teachers and Lecturers (ATL) and the National Union of Teachers (NUT).

Brown, E. D. & Sax, K. L. (2013). Arts enrichment and preschool emotions for low-income children at risk. *Early Childhood Research Quarterly*, 28(2), 337–346.

Bruce, T. (2005). Play, the universe and everything! in Moyles, J. (ed.), *The excellence of play* (2nd edn). Maidenhead: Open University Press.

Catterall, J. S. (1997). Involvement in the arts and success in secondary school. *Americans for the Arts Monographs*, 1(9), 8.

Child of the New Century. Home and Family (2016). Available at: https://childnc.net/what-have-we-learned/home-and-family (accessed 24 November 2017).

Churchill Dower, R., Hogan, S., Hoy, C., & Sims, H. (2006). Search for meaning – The children's curriculum. Bradford: Canterbury Nursery School and Centre for Children and Families.

Cizek, F. (1921). *The child as artist: Some conversations with Professor Cizek.* London: Children's Art Exhibition Fund.

CLA Collective (2012). ImagiNation – *A case for cultural learning.* London: Cultural Learning Alliance, pp. 2–4.

Clark, J., Griffiths, C., & Taylor H. (2003). *Feeding the mind, valuing the arts in the development of young children.* Newcastle: Arts Council England, North East.

Csikszentmihalyi, M. (1996). *Creativity – flow and the psychology of discovery and invention.* New York: HarperCollins.

Development Matters in the Early Years Foundation Stage (EYFS): Non-statutory guidance material to support practitioners in implementing the statutory requirements of the EYFS (2012). London: British Association of Early Childhood Educators. Available at: https://www.foundationyears.org.uk/files/2012/03/Development-Matters-FINAL-PRINT-AMENDED.pdf (accessed 23 August 2017).

Duffy, B. (2006). *Supporting creativity and imagination in the early years.* Oxford: Oxford University Press.

Duffy, B. (2010). Using creativity and creative learning to enrich the lives of young children at the Thomas Coram Centre, in Tims, C. (ed.), *Born creative*, London: Demos, pp. 19–28.

Elias, C. L. & Berk, L. E. (2002). Self-regulation in young children: Is there a role for socio-dramatic play? *Early Childhood Research Quarterly*, 17(2), 216–238.

Ellyatt, W. (2010). A science of learning: new approaches to thinking about creativity in the early years, in Tims, C. (ed.), *Born creative*, London: Demos, pp. 89–98.

Goddard Blythe, S. (2004). *The well balanced child: Movement and early learning* (revised edn). Stroud: Hawthorne Press.

Grace, J. (2018). *Sensory being for sensory beings: Creating entrancing sensory experiences.* Oxon: Routledge.

Heath, S. & Wolf, S. (2005). Focus in creative learning: Drawing on art for language development. Literacy, 39(1), 38–45.

Hood, P. (2017). *The never-ending story of EYFS assessment.* University of Nottingham. http://bit.ly/2zskr3p (accessed 8 November 2017).

Ipsos Mori (2009). Parents' views on creative and cultural education. London: CCE.

Jayatilaka, G. (2010). Creative futures: a 'new deal' for the early years sector in Tims, C. (ed.), Born creative, London: Demos, pp. 71–82.

Landry, C. & Bianchini, F. (2012). *The creative city: A toolkit for urban innovators*. London: Demos, p. 21.

Lonie, D. (2010). *Early years evidence review: Assessing the outcomes of early years music making*. London: Youth Music.

Mualem, O. & Klein, P. S. (2013). The communicative characteristics of musical interactions compared with play interactions between mothers and their one-year-old infants. *Early Child Development and Care*, 183(7), 1–17.

Muñiz, E. I., Silver, E. J., & Stein, R. E. K. (2014). Family routines and social-emotional school readiness among preschool-age children. *Journal of Developmental & Behavioural Paediatrics*, 35, 93–99.

'Music for Change' 2015–18 – *Collaborating with Speech and Language Therapists: a multi-perspective report*. Available from: https://www.researchgate.net/publication/309033022_%27Music_for_Change%27_2015-18_Collaborating_with_Speech_and_Language_Therapists_a_multi-perspective_report (accessed 24 November 2017).

NACCCE (National Advisory Committee on Creative and Cultural Education), Robinson, K. (ed.) (1999). All our futures: Creativity, culture and education. Report to the Secretary of State for Education and Employment and the Secretary of State for Culture, Media and Sport.

National Children's Bureau (NCB) (2010). *Principles for engaging with families*: A framework for local authorities and national organisations to evaluate and improve engagement with families. London: NCB.

O'Connor, A. & Daly, A. (2016). *Understanding physical development in the early years: Linking bodies and minds*. Oxon: Routledge.

Oskala, A. et al. (2009). *Encourage children today to build audiences for tomorrow: Evidence from the Taking Part survey on how childhood involvement in the arts affects arts engagement in adulthood*. London: Arts Council England.

Pennebaker, J. (2004). *Writing to heal: A guided journal for recovering trauma and emotional upheaval*. Oakland, CA: New Harbinger Publications.

Perkins, S. & Orly, R. (1999). *Seeing, making, doing*: Creative development in early years. Dundee: Scottish Consultative Council on the Curriculum, p. 37.

Pink, D. H. (2006). *A whole new mind: Why right-brainers will rule the future*. London: Cyan Books, p. 1.

Rinaldi, C. (2001). Parents and robotics: The courage of Utopia, in Guidici, C., Rinaldi, C., & Krechevsky, M. (eds), *Making learning visible: Children as individual and group learners*. Reggio Emilia: Project Zero, Harvard Graduate School of Education, pp. 148–151.

Robinson, K. (2007). *Do Schools Kill Creativity?* Ted Talk. https://www.youtube.com/watch?v=iG9CE55wbtY (accessed 24 August 2017).

Robinson, K. (2012). *Keynote Presentation at the Earlyarts UnConference 2012*. https://vimeo.com/53456183 (accessed 24 August 2017).

Rosen, M. (2010). *Foreword* in Tims, C. (ed.), *Born creative*. London: Demos, pp. 9–11.

Schore, A. N. & Marks-Tarlow, T. (2017). How love opens creativity, play and the arts through early right brain development, in Marks-Tarlow, T., Siegel, D. J., & Solomon, M. (eds), *Play and creativity in psychotherapy (Norton Series on Interpersonal Neurobiology)*, New York: W.W. Norton.

Siraj-Blatchford, I. et al. (2002). Researching effective pedagogy in the early years. London: Department for Education and Skills.

Sousa, D. (2006). *How the arts develop the brain*. The School Superintendents Association, www.aasa.org/SchoolAdministratorArticle.aspx (accessed 31 August 2017).

Vygotsky, L. (1978). Interaction between learning and development, in Gauvain, M. & Cole, M. (eds), *Readings on the development of children*. New York: Scientific American Books, p. 38.

Witkin, R. (1974). The intelligence of feeling. Harlow: Heinemann Educational Publishers.

Wood, D., Bruner, J., & Ross, G. (1976). The role of tutoring in problem solving. *Journal of Child Psychology and Psychiatry and Allied Disciplines*, 17, 89–100.

White, R., Lord, P., & Sharp, C. (2015). *Headteachers' perspectives on the In Harmony programme*. London: NFER.

10

AN INTERNATIONAL DIMENSION

Making a world of difference

Helen Wright

A young child in the UK today inhabits a vastly different world from the world of 1994, when Sir Christopher Ball wrote his seminal report, *Start Right: The Importance of Early Learning* (Ball, 1994). Horizons have enlarged, society has evolved, and the explosion of digital technology has connected people locally, nationally and internationally as never before.

Since 1994, the world has grown. From a global population of 5.7 billion in 1995, the number of people inhabiting our planet had expanded to 7.4 billion by 2016, and continues to rise. Although many people speak English as a second language, our children live in a world where more people (14.1 per cent of the world's population) speak Chinese as a first language, or Spanish (5.85 per cent) than English (5.52 per cent). If our children are to prepare for a life in the wider world, they need to learn to appreciate the linguistic, cultural and geographical diversity within this world.

This will be brought home to many children in the UK because since 1994 migration patterns – for reasons ranging from fleeing war to the search for economic prosperity – have multiplied, and the composition of the make-up of the UK population has started to shift as a result. According to the UK Office for National Statistics, the 'white ethnic' group accounted for 86 per cent of the usual resident population in the UK in 2011, a decrease from 91.3 per cent in 2001 and 94.1 per cent in 1991. Different parts of the UK have different degrees of ethnic diversity, with London topping the table, but there can be no denying that our children are growing up in an increasingly ethnically diverse society.

Moreover – and perhaps most importantly - our children (and even our youngest children) are closer to the wider world than ever before. In 1995, only 7 per cent of the UK population had mobile phones; today there are more phones than people, and 80 per cent of these are smartphones. Globally, there were 2.1 billion smartphones in use in 2015, and this is predicted to rise to 6.1 billion by 2020.

According to a study by US-based Common Sense Media in 2013 (Rideout, 2013), 72 per cent of children age 8 and under had used a mobile device for some type of media activity such as playing games, watching videos or using apps, up from 38 per cent in 2011, while 38 per cent of children under 2 had used a mobile device for media (compared with 10 per cent two years before). Children are surrounded by technology that provides them with easy access to resources and information – and people – from all over the world, in a way that is genuinely unprecedented.

With technology and accessibility has come a flood of images and messages to which children have become exposed as never before. The Bailey Review in 2011 on the sexualisation and commercialisation of childhood, *Letting Children Be Children* (Bailey, 2011) wrote of the 'wallpaper' of children's lives as increasingly sexualised and commercialised, not least because of the sheer volume of stimuli to which children are exposed in the media, online, in adverts at bus-stops and so on. The report, which proposed a number of practical regulatory suggestions to help establish boundaries to enable children to grow without undue influence, also made the case for a balanced approach moving forward:

> We recognise that the issues raised by the commercialisation and sexualisa-tion of childhood are rooted in the character of our wider adult culture and that children need both protection from a range of harms, and knowledge of different kinds, appropriate to their age, understanding and experience.
>
> *(Bailey, 2011, p. 10)*

In other words, there is no turning back of the clock to a (probably idealised) past in which children were gloriously unaware of the world around them, and this is a crucial realisation for Early Years teachers and leaders. We cannot hold the world back, but we can help shape our children's understanding of this world, and – more than ever before – this is perhaps our prime responsibility.

Of course, this is especially pertinent when we consider that technology will have another significant impact on the future lives of our young children: as a result of all these advances in technology, the kind of work that our children will eventually under-take will most likely be very different from what work looks like now. According to McKinsey Global Institute, (Manyika et al., 2013), it is estimated that by 2025, robots may have replaced between 25 million and 40 million jobs in developed countries and between 15 million and 35 million in developing countries. In 2016, the World Economic Forum acknowledged that it was likely that 65 per cent of primary school children today would end up working in completely new job types that do not yet exist (Leopold et al., 2016). Work is changing – and this brings with it the opportunity to rethink, radically, what children today might need to do and learn in school, from their earliest years onwards, in order to be able to lead self-sustaining lives in the future.

The world has shifted since 1995, and it continues to shift; technological innova-tion underpins these changes, and it is probably fair to say that it will continue to do so, in ways that many of us cannot even imagine yet. In fact, probably the only certainty about the future for the young children embarking upon an Early Years education this year is that it will be uncertain. How, then, can we conceptualise the kind of education that they will need? Interestingly, in amongst these fundamental shifts in our connections with the wider world since 1994, educational thinking has also evolved. Increasingly powerful voices such as Sir Ken Robinson and Professor Yong Zhao are echoing the philosophies of the progressive, post-industrial, educational thinkers of the early twentieth century – Dewey, Montessori, Parkhurst – when they point out that an unfortunate by-product of striving to provide equality of access to education for all children has been a tightening of the stranglehold of standardised assessment in schools and school systems.

Standardised assessment does precisely what the term indicates – it standardises, by comparing all children with a pre-determined average. In his book, *The End of Average* (Rose, 2016), the author relates a telling anecdote about how the US Air Force carefully designed their pilot seats based on scores of data about the human shape, ensuring that it was the perfect average, only to discover that no pilot was the perfect average. Success rates of missions soared once the seats were made adjustable, so that the pilots could respond to the controls from a position that was unique and individual to them. The answer, as we will explore later in this chapter, lies in greater individualisation of education, greater personalisation, and greater focus on strengths-based learning.

The young Early Years teachers of today were children in 1995. They have grown up in a world that was less diverse, less technologically connected and more focused on standardisation in education than the world today. It is inevitable that they will have been marked by their own experiences, and they need help to challenge themselves – and their children – to reach out and grasp the opportunities that the wider world presents. What, then, should they be teaching their children about the wider world, and how should they be approaching this task? These questions form the basis of the rest of the chapter.

What should we be teaching our youngest children?

In answering this question, we need to ask ourselves what our children need in order to be able to thrive in a connected, diverse world. It is not sufficient for Early Years educators to focus only on the self, the family and the immediate local community, passing responsibility for an introduction to the international world further up the school. For even the youngest children, the global world either already is their world – because of the exposure they have had to different languages, cultures and perspectives – or it should be part of their world, because the values and experiences that young children encounter are instrumental in shaping their fundamental understanding of the world and their own future potential within it. It is incumbent upon Early Years educators to lead this.

With this in mind, four key areas move to centre stage for the Early Years Educator:

1   *Universal values, tolerance and appreciation of diversity*: Understanding self and understanding others: this has long been a focus of the Early Years teacher.

Schools have a powerful – and socially mandated – role to play in developing the values of children. The process of discussing, exploring and teaching values has often elicited ethical tensions in education, especially when values from different cultures seem to conflict, but when seen through the lens of ensuring that children learn to value everyone in the world – all 7.5 billion of them – teachers need to remember that they have recourse to the values frameworks that govern international relationships.

These are encapsulated in the words of the United Nations Universal Declaration of Human Rights, which is effectively the closest that the human race has to a shared set of values. The Universal Declaration of Human Rights has stood the test of time (it was signed in 1948) and yet while there are a number of child-friendly versions in existence, work still needs to be done to interpret it so that it is meaningful to young children. Every aspect of this Universal Declaration is relevant to children; young children, for example, are no longer isolated from concepts such as war and violence, because they see this around them in the home, online and on the front of newspapers when they go shopping with their parents. Early Years teachers have a responsibility to help interpret the world for children, and not simply shut it out of the classroom.

How teachers live, model, highlight and develop the universal values that connect all of humanity will in all likelihood not be far removed from what they are doing already to facilitate positive relationships between children, but when done with an awareness of an international context, it opens up numerous opportunities to help children understand that there is a wider world, and that while people beyond the boundaries of their classroom, school and local community may be different, they are also essentially the same. World maps, globes, a chart of the solar system and world clocks (with time zones – an interesting concept to explore), as well as different means of transport including ships and planes: all of these should be staples of the Early Years classroom, as indeed could be connections with other children in other schools across the world. Children can build relationships across international boundaries through technology already readily available to schools (real-time video conferencing, with translation if necessary); when new technologies such as virtual reality come online, they may offer new possibilities. What really matters is that children are able to learn, from an early age, that people live in different parts of the world, in different geographical and cultural conditions, speaking different languages, but can still connect (and can enjoy playing with the same toys).

2   *Linguistic awareness and capability:* Language is a key differentiating factor between people from different cultures, and the Early Years classroom offers the potential for children to become exposed to different languages at an early age. Research into bilingualism in children increasingly indicates that bilingual children often experience a cognitive advantage that enhances their ability to solve problems; and although the evidence for a 'critical period' in second language learning is less secure than for first language learning, numerous research

studies, including those from the Cornell University Language Acquisition Lab (Yang & Lust, 2009), indicate that learning a second language at an early age does not cause 'language confusion, language delay or cognitive deficit'. On the contrary, in fact, multiple research studies have shown that children who learn a second language are better than children who know only one language at maintaining attention when they encounter outside stimuli – an outcome which implies that these children are better positioned to learn other skills in and beyond school. Language learning – preferably in an immersion context – really is possible (and even desirable) for young children.

More broadly, of course, linguistic competence is essential for connection in the wider world. The learning of languages in secondary school may have dropped in popularity since 1995 for a number of reasons (not least a perceived lack of relevance by young people), but with the gradual diminishing of English as a first language in the world, today's children are limiting their opportunities if they do not at least appreciate the value of learning language. This begins with understanding that different languages exist, seeing language learning as normal, and then experimenting with other languages. This kind of learning is eminently possible within the Early Years classroom – and, arguably, it is the responsibility of Early Years teachers to start children on this journey.

3   *Digital literacy*: 'Screen time' is an emotive subject at home and in school. Over the past few years concerns have been raised from a number of quarters about the amount of time that young children (from birth) are exposed to electronic entertainment instead of engaging in social interaction and physical play. Any evidence of harm, however, is inconclusive, and appears (unsurprisingly) to be connected with over-use, or the side-effects of its use e.g. a more sedentary childhood. Using technology can be an advantage too, and develop different skills. Given that technology (and not just screen-based technology) is now established as a part of the lives of children – and assuming, too, that common sense dictates the use of technology as part of a balanced education pattern that includes fresh air, movement, tactile play and social interaction – then the opportunity exists in the Early Years classroom for teachers to build the confidence of children in the use of technology.

In practice, this means a number of different things, including building familiarity with technology and its many current forms – playing with robotics, for example, basic coding for slightly older children, and online games. It also involves helping children imagine what technology might or could do, and giving them access to real-life tools perhaps previously reserved for older children in more specialised courses – actual computers to disassemble, for instance, or electronic components to pull apart and reconnect with other play materials. In the same way that we are happy to give children a blank piece of paper and pencils, with a range of learning intents including the development of basic motor skills and the stretching of their creativity, so too should we be prepared to give children access to the equivalent in blank technological canvases. Genuine experimentation is the goal – not just the circumscribed experimentation of pre-determined, standardised, 'age-appropriate' experiments of 'age-appropriate' activity workbooks. Teachers are going to have to be bold – and child-led.

Similarly, young children can be encouraged to experiment and feel comfortable with different forms of interactive communications technology – eminently possible when there are strong web filters in place. For years, young children have played with cups and string in order to talk to one another across rooms; taking this a few steps further into learning how to connect with other children in other classrooms across the world via video conferencing is a natural extension.

4   *Resilience, creativity and adaptability*: In an uncertain world, with a future that will most likely exceed the bounds of our current expectations, one of the most significant ways in which we can help children grow into successful, happy adults is to help them develop their independence and sense of self. Integral to this is the ability to be resilient, curious, creative, flexible and adaptable – and while children are often all of these, it is up to the teacher (together with all the other significant adults in a child's life) to nurture these and ensure that they are not squeezed out of the child as he/she progresses through the school. Creating a mistake-friendly environment, where children can be challenged, learn to work independently and collaboratively, and develop their growth mindset rather than become fixed in their approach to success and failure ... all of these are the task of the Early Years teacher.

Bringing the global into the Early Years classroom is not just a 'nice-to-have' or an 'add-on' for children who need to be extended; baldly and boldly, it is actually about the ability of these children to survive in today's world. We talk often in education about the worrying (and increasing) attainment gap between rich and poor children, and we focus on teaching them basic skills and preparing them for standardised tests and examinations. We worry about getting all the building blocks in place before we dare to introduce concepts such as the wider world, and subconsciously perhaps we believe that children who 'struggle' in school to progress according to pre-determined norms or adhere to the order of the classroom will have less use for an international understanding than other, more compliant children. Suppose, though, we turned this understanding on its head ... suppose we realised that for children from all backgrounds (but perhaps especially from backgrounds of disadvantage) access to the global world is a fundamental component of their future social mobility. Suppose we recognised that for them, being able to love inventing with technology, and finding ways to communicate with different people, will be as essential for their ability to sustain themselves in later life as their ability to read and write, and that an awareness of the wider world and its immense diversity will underpin this ... surely, then, we would make sure that this was embedded, visible and resounding in all our activities in the Early Years classroom.

Change starts with realising what needs to change, and Early Years teachers are at the forefront of imagining what this could be.

How can Early Years teachers help their children learn all these skills and dispositions?

1 Focus on the child; a child-centred education

Professor Yong Zhao (Zhao, 2012) argues that in a connected world, everyone has a potential role to play, and a means of earning a living, because someone, somewhere, will need and want what they have and can do. This means that we need to shed our fear that children will not be prepared for the world if they do not emerge with a university degree and a string of academic qualifications. While we need to be very, very careful that this does not lead to teachers lowering aspirations for children who present as less traditionally school-able than others (often because they have come from a position of socio-economic or other disadvantage), it does mean that if teachers seek to nurture individuality and the unique profiles of children, helping them to become less average (remember that pilot's seat) and more distinctive, then they are more likely to be able to find a place in the wider world later on.

Child-centred learning is not straightforward, however; it requires considerable rigour, patience and courage for educators to enable, encourage and empower young children to learn, grow and develop from a position of who they are as individuals, not according to a shared (and standardised) understanding of who all children 'should' be. Luckily, there is over a century's worth of writing and research into how to facilitate children's learning. As highlighted in Chapter 2, Early Years teachers who delve into the archives and re-read the work of the progressive educationalists of the 1920s will be richly rewarded.

2 Create space within the EYFS requirements; and further down the line in schools

Without space, time and resources, it is hard for teachers to allow children genuinely to learn at their own pace, following their own passions, and developing in their own unique directions. Even when an EYFS environment is fervently committed to play-based learning, the requirements that teachers have to ensure that children meet can frequently skew the experience of the child, who, rather than being guided by the teacher, ends up being led. EYFS teachers need longer to be able to help children shape their own pathways, and they certainly should not be handing children over to a different approach to learning, exploration and discovery at the age of 5.

3 Upskill in three key areas: understanding, language and digital skills

Fundamental to the ability to help young children thrive in a global world is the belief that the global is as important as the local in educating, even in the earliest years. If a teacher does not believe this, then he/she will not translate it into the choices he/she makes in the classroom. It is, therefore, absolutely essential that teachers begin from this perspective, and grow in their own awareness of how the wider world already impacts on the lives of their students, and how this impact is likely to increase, so that they can become absolutely committed to helping their students navigate this world.

Second, Early Years teachers need to learn more languages. Partly this is so that they can appreciate the value of learning languages, and can gain access to the cultural diversity that language learning releases, and partly it is so that they are learning alongside their students, as co-learners. Obviously, it also makes it easier for teachers to introduce languages into the classroom if they already have an awareness of a range of languages. There is also a real place for specialist teachers of languages in the EY classroom, both to support bilingual or trilingual children, and to normalise and encourage language learning amongst all children.

Third, Early Years teachers need to spend time (which translates as 'be given time') exploring the potential of the digital world, so that they can bring this safely and with confidence into the classroom. Ultimately, the goal of an Early Years teacher is not to teach children how to use technology, but rather it is to facilitate the children's own exploration of its potential, and the purpose of upskilling in this area is not to become proficient in the usage of specific tools, but instead to develop curiosity and imagination, learning to ask the 'what if?' and 'why not?' questions. Why can't children take apart robotic toys and then try to create new ones? Why can't they chat to other children in Hong Kong, Denver, France or Malawi whose classrooms are permanently linked via video-conferencing screens in the corner of the classroom? What if …?

A child's imagination is boundless; a teacher's can be too.

Conclusion

As the various contributors to this volume have shown, the time has come to revise early childhood education. The new framework proposed by Preedy in Chapter 2 provides coherence from birth to age 7 years – truly covering the stage of early childhood. It encompasses the areas of learning explored in this book focusing firmly on the individual child and his or her family. It is true that Preedy has retained standardised testing alongside the proposed curriculum – we still need to prove that high achievement is because of, not in spite of an holistic approach to learning. This is new territory, as the possibilities offered by technology continue to proliferate, but there are equally strong pathways laid out in the chapters of this book that build on research, educational thought and – in many cases – common sense about how to bring up children to become well-balanced human beings.

There is a world of opportunity for young people ahead of them; it is up to us to help them find it, access it, and thrive in it, and we can – and should – start right in their earliest years.

References

Bailey, R. (2011). *Letting Children Be Children.* London: HMSO.

Ball, C. (1994). *Start Right: The Importance of Early Learning.* London: RSA.

Leopold, T., Ratcheva, V. & Zahidid, S. (2016). *The Future of Jobs Report.* Switzerland: World Economic Forum.

Manyika, J., Chui, M., Bughin, J., Dobbs, R., Bisson, P. & Marrs, A. (2013). *Disruptive Technologies: Advances that Will Transform Life, Business and the Global Economy.* San Francisco, CA: McKinsey Global Institute.

Rideout, V. (2013). *Zero to Eight: Children's Media Use in America 2013.* San Francisco, CA: Common Sense.

Rose, T. (2016). *The End of Average: How We Succeed in a World that Values Sameness.* New York: HarperOne.

Yang, S. & Lust, B. (2009). *Discovering Child Language and Cognitive Growth.* Ithaca, NY: Cornell University.

Zhao, Y. (2012). *World Class Learners. Educating Creative and Entrepreneurial Students.* London: Sage.

11

CONCLUSION – SO WHAT?

Sir Christopher Ball

That question ('So what, Daddy?') was one our youngest child used to ask after a parental sermon on improvement! It is a good question, and one we should try to answer at the end of this book. I suggested in Chapter 1 that we (our society and government – and profession) needed to readdress three substantial issues in the early provision for our children's learning: the education and training of parents, the curriculum appropriate for 0–7-year-olds (What should they be learning and being taught?), and the pedagogy (How may they best learn it, and how best can we teach, support and help them?). If that's the agenda, who should do what by when? – (my version of Richard's question).

On the issue of parental education, we suggest that the first step is to stimulate a national (even global?) debate on the subject. This will require the commitment and leadership of those in positions of authority and responsibility throughout our society: members of the Royal Family, perhaps, the Prime Minister and Cabinet, politicians of all parties, religious and community leaders, charities, professional bodies and charitable organisations such as *Save the Children, Family Lives, Twins and Multiple Births Association* and the *Marriage Foundation*. The questions are:

1   What are the essential qualities of the competent parent?
2   How may we ensure that everyone who chooses parenthood (or has it thrust upon them) develops and sustains these qualities?
3   What does good practice look like? The acronym NESTLE that I describe in Chapter 1 offers a starting point for the debate.

It is interesting to note how many of the contributors to this book have picked up, developed and emphasised the importance of *attachment* and *nurture* (in its widest sense), *exercise* (Outdoor Education is, sadly, the Cinderella of the British system today), *love* (defined precisely as *acceptance, care, trust, stimulation* (especially of the creative imagination), *talk* (language and intelligence are what define our species), and the *environment* (especially the external world of nature and the open air) in which our children are raised and spend their formative years. In Chapter 3 Sally Goddard Blythe underlines the importance of movement as the child's first *A, B, C*. Ignorance of this area of child development has allowed the modern world to impact adversely on many children and families as described in Chapters 4 (*Movement for Learning Project*) and Chapter 6 (*Play Partners Project*).

An early win might be achieved by providing all early years teachers and practitioners with training, leading to an appropriate qualification in the provision of courses (and support) for parents in effective parenting and parental engagement focused on their children's learning. The key point is the urgent need to strengthen and improve parental education and training for the sake of our children and grandchildren (and theirs).

In Chapter 2 Professor Preedy sets out a suggested revised curriculum for Key Stage 1, the framework for learning (and teaching) for children aged 0–7. This provides an imaginative solution to the long-standing problem, identified in the *Start Right* Report, that the UK's practice of starting the formal curriculum at 5 – and in many cases the *rising fives* are still some months short of their fifth birthday – is not only out of line with what is evidently good practice in many other nations, but also clearly detrimental to the later educational progress and success (and the consequent life-chances) of many children. Hot-housing may work for some children in some families, but it is not a good idea for incorporation into a national system of education. What (and how) we expect our children to learn should be planned in relation to the stages of their brain development, the rate of which differs in different children. Few are ready for Hamlet or long division at the age of 5 – though some may be! As Shakespeare wrote, *the readiness is all*.

This book proposes that early years practitioners, teachers in nursery and primary schools, the Department of Education, Ofsted and the Independent Schools Inspectorate give serious consideration to the case for establishing a new Key Stage 1 for 0–7-year-olds, as outlined here. Without the double approval of those in authority and the professional practitioners, together with the support of parents, it has always proved difficult to introduce educational reforms (however worthy they may seem to be) into our deeply conservative educational system. The challenge for aspiring reformers is twofold: to be right, and to be effective. We invite those who are more expert and experienced than we are to consider whether this proposal is the right one (or, at least, a good deal better than the inert status quo). But we shall need the support and co-operation of all concerned (government, educators and parents) to effect the real and beneficial changes we seek.

It is encouraging to see that the basic principles set out in the *Start Right* Report in 1994 are still thought to be sound and appropriate for planning a system of teaching and learning for the young child. Professor Preedy's revised Key Stage 1 curriculum builds on these principles and also takes careful account of the research and informed reflection of the last 24 years. It is also sensitive to the social changes that have occurred, and which will continue to affect the context for early learning and child-care. In summary, we recommend the following:

1   A renewed commitment to the principles of early childhood education set out in *the Start Right* Report of 1994;
2   The replacement of the Early Years Foundation Stage with a new Key Stage 1 covering 0–7 years (Kindergarten 0–2; Nursery 2–4; Reception 4–5; Years One and Two 5–7), which will enable a smooth progression to Key Stage 2 and integration into later Key Stages;
3   A careful updating of the curriculum for early learning originally developed by Professor Kathy Sylva in the *Start Right* Report of 1994, p. 104.
4.   Replace the Early Years Foundation Stage Profile (EYFSP) with a combination of teacher/practitioner assessment used for planning and standardised assessments in language, mathematics and physical development.

The third issue of concern for us is pedagogy. We hold out little hope that the community at large or its alternative governments will be likely to address this issue during our lifetime: obsession with the curriculum is endemic. But we appeal to the profession we are all proud to serve (or have served) to begin at last to give due attention to the science (and art) of pedagogy: the experience of teaching has led me to believe that what people learn depends not a little on how they are taught. Indeed, I argue that the *how* governs the *what*. In Chapter 1, I invited the education profession to do five things:

1   To re-engage with the realm of pedagogy;
2   To reclaim the challenge of *learning disorders* from medicine;
3   To *redefine the* concept of *learning readiness*;
4   To learn to be sceptical of genetic explanations of *talent* (or its apparent absence);
5   To help all learners understand (and nurture, and exploit) the extraordinary potential of their remarkable brains – and therefore the infinite possibilities of learning.

The later chapters of this book make a number of specific and valuable contributions to each of these concerns: parenting, the early years curriculum and pedagogy. I particularly welcome the emphasis on *purposeful play*, the new (to me) concept of *planning in the moment* and the over-riding concern that all practitioners should be helped to understand the nature and complexity of child-development, the importance of the theory of attachment, and the ways in which young children (and older ones, and adults) learn. Indeed, I look forward to the day – and hope to live to see it – when *brain science* (not brain mythology) will become a foundation subject in the curriculum, alongside numeracy and literacy, for us all.

To seek to change a system of education is probably even more difficult than altering course in a battleship or a super-tanker: neither is easily manoeuvred. But there are two features of systems of education, fundamental to British education but found world-wide (since so much of global education was developed from the

British model, for better or worse), that need to be squarely confronted in a book of this kind: assessment and funding. Both are complex, and we shall not begin to do justice to either topic. But, to facilitate the changes proposed in this book, we need to adapt the existing national system of education in two important ways.

The first is assessment. Educators have long made a distinction between two forms of assessment of students: formative and summative assessment. Both are necessary: one is benign, the other can be a threat to good learning. Formative assessment is what any good teacher does in order to provide helpful feedback to the learner; it typically answers the questions: What went well? What might have been done better? How could it be improved? Formative assessment has one aim – to help the learner, and it is normally a private communication. Most learners welcome it; confident learners always want more! (One of the tasks of the good teacher is to foster confident learning.)

In contrast, summative assessment is mainly designed to inform others of the progress of learning: it is public and *goes on the record* to help in future selection of students for more advanced study or employment. A-levels and university degree classes are obvious examples of summative assessment in the British system (and elsewhere). It is normal (though not requisite) for summative assessments to be made by independent examiners, rather than by the teachers responsible for the preparation of the students (as in A-levels) or by a combination of teachers and externals (as in most university degrees). Summative assessment is one of the most important ways that public education is made accountable to society, its government and the Treasury. It is obviously necessary, but (since it can disrupt good learning) we need to ask how much is enough? I believe that the system has become overloaded with summative assessments: perhaps the time has come to dispense with the GCSE (and replace it with nothing!).

However, given the concern of this book with the early years, we want to suggest the ending of the Early Years Foundation Stage Profile (EYFSP) and replacing it with standardised assessments in literacy, numeracy and physical development from the start of the Reception Year (age 4 to 5 years). The Centre for Evaluation and Monitoring (University of Durham) has over many years developed value added assessments and is now working towards including assessment of physical development based upon research including that detailed in Chapter 4. Teachers would then be able to focus on formative assessment to plan children's learning in partnership with parents and carers. A carefully constructed inspection framework is required in order to ensure that excellent holistic provision is both the expectation and requirement.

Many books and reports have been written on the contentious subject of the funding of systems of education. Governments and taxpayers are justifiably concerned to seek value for money; those who serve in the public sector often feel that the funding is inadequate. Though tempted, we do not wish to add this debate here. We seek to make a more fundamental point: that a good system of education must be *built from the youngest children upwards*. Advising a developing country some years ago, where the President wished to establish a university, I argued that the first priority was primary education: indeed *Save the Children* has recommended that the first essential of development is to teach mothers and children literacy – from which all else will follow.

The *RSA rule of thumb* for the design of a successful system of education is dramatically simple: take the age of the child, double it and treat that number as the appropriate *class-size* for the age-group: 3-year-olds should be in groups of no more than six per adult; 6-year-olds in classes of 12; 12-year-olds in classes of no more than 24, and so on. Such a system would transfer resources from the expensive education of our sixth-formers (and universities) to the early learning of young children. It would enable our society to recruit a well-trained, highly qualified and high-quality workforce for the early years: 'high quality provision is essential to the provision of good early learning' (*Start Right*, p. 7). While it would probably cost no more than the current model, it would yield a far better return since (nearly) all children would, in principle, be enabled to start right, would become effective, independent learners (needing less and less pedagogic support as they matured) and become successful in learning, work and life. I believe that this is a realisable dream: the status quo, we must always remember, is merely one of the options. Perhaps the independent sector in partnership with the state sector could provide a pilot study along these lines?

Reference

Ball, C. (1994). *Start Right: The Importance of Early Learning.* London: RSA.

INDEX